GOD'S BIG ACRE

GOD'S

Life in 401 Country

BIG ACRE

Photography by John Reeves GEORGE ELLIOTT

ⓝ Methuen

TORONTO NEW YORK LONDON SYDNEY AUCKLAND

Canadian Cataloguing in Publication Data

Elliott, George, 1923–
    God's big acre

ISBN 0-458-80400-2

1. Ontario – Description and travel – 1981– I. Title

FC3067.5.E44 1986   917.13′044   C86-093872-7
F1057.E44 1986

Design: The Dragon's Eye Press
Printed and bound in Hong Kong
by Scanner Art Services Inc., Toronto

1 2 3 4 5   86   91 90 89 88 87

CONTENTS

On the way to the museum

INTRODUCTION

401 COUNTRY is a country carefully hidden from the traveller.
There are few exit ramps. It is the prolific space between cities
strung like beads along the 828 kilometres of the four-lane highway.

This utilitarian, no-nonsense highway is the great aorta through
which much of the country's productivity is pumped. Ever since
Maritime boys followed it to dead-end jobs in a Toronto factory
in the film *Going Down The Road*, ever since Jack Chambers
painted the highway landscape at the Woodstock exit ramp, ever

since Eddy Eastman started singing *Eastbound 401*, it has become a part of the national psyche.

401 country is big; big enough to absorb two natural gas pipelines, a petroleum pipeline, electric power corridors, old highway number 2, the St. Lawrence Seaway, much of a nation's farm wealth, much of a nation's manufacturing wealth. It is big food country, big tourism country, big transportation country.

401 country is what lies behind the blur that is the sideband of your sight while you are driving at 100 km/h between cities. It is where independence and individuality are born and thrive. It is where anonymous city people come from. It is where they go back to, to recover lost identities. City people yearn for an "alternative lifestyle" and believe it can be found somewhere in 401 country. They go to 401 country to do all the simple things that are impossible to do in cities, cities where people jam together for the mystical joys and sorrows of compression. Only in the country can birds, blossoms and seasons be truly watched. Only in a cold, narrow, deep, fast-flowing stream can trout be hooked and played. Only in the country can the good old days be realized, in the imagination of nostalgic city people.

The people in 401 country are candid, open-minded, self-reliant and defiant of the odds. They don't feel computerized, dehumanized, automated, straight-jacketed, regimented, stapled, folded or mutilated. When governments start to lean on them, they quickly lean back.

No matter how big the bank loan gets, no matter what the new deductions from the Milk Marketing Board cheque may be, they are in control of big enterprises which they *own*. Owning makes the difference.

They are a competitive, high-tech crowd in 401 country. They can be as nostalgic as the next guy, but there's a computer in the office in the barn; there's a two-year diploma or a four-year degree in a frame back at the house.

They live physical lives. There's no such thing as a fat dairy farmer. There's no such thing as a fat beef farmer. Every day they burn off whatever it is that accumulates around the middle of urban, pear-shaped middle management.

They envy urban nine-to-five-ism. They envy city people, especially on Friday nights at the start of long holiday weekends. The camper, the trailer and boat, the van with the windsurfer on top, they all seem like a better idea than the 400-horsepower Case with eight six-foot wheels and a loan at the bank. They envy but they don't turn green. A lifetime of ownership beats short hours of salaried dependency every time.

There was a time when they mourned the passing of the 100-acre family farm with a dozen milk cows, some sows, a bit of an orchard, a big garden, some fall wheat, corn and barley, the neat little bank barn, a trim house in white board and batten. But now the idea of a different kind of family farm has taken over. Bigger, it demands partnerships of the generations to manage it successfully.

In Stormont, in Northumberland, in Oxford, in Essex, wholesome dynasties are emerging on farms where Mom and Dad have the neat new split-level on the corner, number one son is in the original homestead, number two son (or a daughter and son-in-law) has the old brick house up the road. Grandchildren are coming along and they know they are going to do what Dad's doing now, what Grandpa did in his time. They have their dreams.

I went looking for the man from 401 country and found him and his family – generous and candid – in every county across which the 401 unravels. There was no rhyme or reason for my route. An uncalculated randomness took me from person to person, from place to place, from farm to farm.

The first part of my search began at the Quebec border and ended ambiguously in the Metro Toronto Zoo. The second part started on the Ambassador Bridge in Windsor and finished nostalgically in the Ontario Agricultural Museum in Milton.

In the stretches between the border and the zoo, between the bridge and the museum, I found fathers and mothers and sons and daughters coalescing in rewarding business relationships, putting in long hours and not concealing their pride in their achievements, their independence, their rugged individualism.

This book is for and about those people.

ON THE WAY TO THE ZOO

Earle Chatten, Northumberland County.

1   *The Man from 401 Country*

THERE ARE NO BULGING HIPS, no sagging behind, no pen-
dulous pot belly hanging over his belt buckle. He is lean
like a champion tennis player. He doesn't drink or smoke, doesn't
stay up late nights. He weighs the same now as he did in grade
twelve. He knew all along that he had the choice of staying

home to help run the farm with his father or leaving home to do something else. The choice was easy for him and he has never regretted it.

After high school he went to the nearest college of agricultural technology for two years and got his diploma. He goofed off a little during his years at Kemptville; nothing wild or embarrassing.

He tried a few things after he graduated. He went to teachers' college for a year and taught in a public school for two years. He worked for a Chrysler dealership in town for two years; was a field man for Pioneer one year; but the homestead was strong in his memory. So he made a deal that gives his father an easier life in "semi-retirement" and that gives him the means to assume, bit by bit, full ownership of the farming operation he watched his father build.

He married a girl he met at Junior Farmers. No, no, they were at the district high together. She gave up nursing to become his wife. You watch, she'll be back to part-time nursing after the kids grow up. He is happily married, in his mid-forties, hoping he is doing as good a job with their three children as he figures his parents did with him.

When he and his father first sat down to talk about how it could be between them, how ownership would move from one generation to the next, how decisions would be made while both were active, he had some pangs. He was supposed to feel impatient with his father's way of doing things. He was supposed to want to change everything and to start doing it all the way he'd learned at the college. He was supposed to want to expand, get the big bank loans, get all new bigger equipment. The magazine articles and guest lecturers at Ridgetown all told him that was how he was supposed to feel; but he felt none of it. Instead he felt relaxed and reassured. His father had gone to Guelph in his time and had been through all the ups and downs. He was never in a mood to ignore his father's judgement.

Besides, his father made the farm interesting. There may have been some drudgery every day but there was always a reason. His father never talked down to him, never hid things from him.

Oh, he knows he puts in long hours compared with some of the guys who left the family farm to teach or to sell herbicides and pesticides or to become accountants; but he doesn't resent it when the comparison comes up because he is building his ownership of land, livestock, machinery, and sometimes a milk quota. His city friends aren't able to do that on what they can save from their secure salaries. There are twinges of resentment, though, when he thinks about their working hours, paid holidays, long weekends. But only twinges. He is his own boss. What

he has, what they don't have, is a big successful farming operation. It has to be managed carefully and skillfully to support
two or three families, to give his children the best possible education, to give them options, to give his wife and children the
essential luxuries to equal the quality of city life – the VCR, the
dish antenna in the orchard, riding lessons, winter holidays,
skiing, a summer cottage.

The homestead means a lot to him. He has taken as his own
all the warm, and even the imperfect, memories of his mother
and father, of his grandmother and grandfather.

Glen Buchner, Oxford County.

Rod Grant, Stormont County.

Where the creek cuts into the clay bank, where the orchard
used to be, where the winter's wood is piled, where the wild
strawberries grow, his father's mail box, the old drive shed, the
abandoned barn on the next farm, the view from the knoll beside
the silos, the stumps of the row of maple trees that used to shade
the lane, the choke-cherry trees, the clump of ironwood trees,
the rock pile, the foot scraper, the old lilac bushes, the rhubarb

clumps, the surface water well, the colour of earth in Spring after it has been disced, the folds in the land, the powdery wave of corn tassels in August, the arthritic dog that supervises from his usual place on the corner of the lawn – these are the gentle and ineradicable images of permanence and possession. Neither his absence nor his aggravation could ever force them out of his being.

He has concerns about the future. He knows that he and all the other efficient farmers can produce more food than the market can absorb. He would like to produce more; but he must live

Earl Elgie, Kent County.

'Bud' Condie, Glengarry County.

5

with supply management systems on the edge of surpluses, because unexpected declining prices, unexpected rising costs, unexpected changes in foreign supply and demand can bring him to the edge of insolvency in one season.

So a lot of his conversation is about money. He is still paying principal and interest on a beginning farmer's mortgage. He is using the operating line of credit at the bank because, obviously, farm-running expenses always precede the arrival of cash income. Machinery repairs are unpredictable nuisances. The weather – forecast with meticulous inaccuracy – may betray him this Summer and he may have to buy feed to replace the hay or corn that will shrivel in a spell of drought. Commodity prices and markets are like the weather – studied and analyzed by well-educated experts who specialize in forecasting their ups and downs – unpredictable, never to be trusted.

He is cautious in his choice of words. He knows farmers are notorious complainers; but he does not want to be regarded as a nagging whiner. Just the same, he has given his life to the land that needs his care, to the benevolent and destructive whims of the weather, to the sensitivity of intensely bred animals, to the pursuit of noxious weeds and pests that will not die. For him there is no holiday from the routine. Will the crops grow and yield adequately? Will they sell at a good price? Will they convert to animal protein at a profitable rate? Will I lose calves or piglets for God knows what reason? Will the rains hold off for just one more day? Will the fertilizer dealer wait another week? Can I get another year out of this tractor? Will there be enough heat units this Summer?

It is a unique life lived in harmony or discord with natural and man-made variables depending on luck and his own management. He thinks there should be unique rewards.

He is an independent man and guards his independence carefully. He will take his turn on the board of a breeders' association and the county fair; but he doesn't want to act as a spokesman. He never politicks for position. Television cameras don't come to his farm in search of the exotic or the unusual. If anyone asks him to be a candidate for public office he manages to find a reason not to run. In a quiet-spoken way he is a booster for his way of life, his farming specialty, his community, but he just doesn't like to be *visible* about these things.

Sometimes it is hard to persuade him to open up about certain subjects. The trade union movement has its attractions. It can organize and stand up to management; but, well, it seems strange that some of them can get new wage settlements that at least keep them even with inflation – yet a lot of farmers who work harder, longer hours and have more at risk are just scraping by. Strip development should have been stopped long ago. When land is zoned agricultural, leave it that way. Otherwise municipal taxes go up. Unemployment insurance pays so much out in benefits there's no more seasonal labour willing to work. Farmers can't compete with that.

He watches small crossroads villages die out. Four- and even eight-room schools are closed down. Churches are boarded up. Little gas stations and general stores wither and die. The distances he and his family have to travel for school and shopping seem longer every year.

Terry Wright, Essex County.

He does not apologize for bigness. He admits that fewer, bigger farms with bigger machinery have reduced the old sense of community and the tradition of helping one another that his parents grew up on.

He is bemused by city people who believe they can create an economic alternative lifestyle with a few head of beef cattle, or sheep or goats or trees or fruit bushes and a nice vegetable garden

Paul Buchner, Oxford County.

organically fertilized. Bemused but not critical because, after all, 401 country is where the dreamer stands on land that is his own, nourishing himself on a landscape that will not change in his lifetime. It is where there is space enough for the grandest of dreams, time enough for dreams to come true – or to be re-dreamed if the world turns stubborn.

2 *Tunnel without Walls*

Y OU HAVE ONLY ENOUGH TIME to stop for well-meaning food at an isolated Texaco highway centre. You have a schedule to keep, a deadline to meet, a motel to check into before six o'clock or the room will be gone. Only the exit ramp signs tell you of your progress. Nothing tells you of the life between the cities.

Quebec's highway 20 runs straight as an arrow across the flatland of Comte de Soulanges. The 18-wheelers and the busses barrel past *Bienvenue en Ontario* signs and into Glengarry County where 401 country begins.

Far to the left – beyond Lac St. François, beyond Huntingdon County – are the last of the Adirondack Mountains. The land is so flat here the Adirondacks are a distant blue backdrop for most of Glengarry.

"Lancaster flats" is the name given by geologists to this till plain of 160 square miles that straddles the provincial border. It is a corner of the country whose deep mix of sand and clay is flat because it didn't get worked over by the last of four glaciers that advanced and retreated across Ontario. Those were the glaciers that pulverized southern Ontario into 20,000,000 acres of almost uninterrupted productivity. They left behind them small subtleties like the Lancaster flats but they also created two major disturbances: the Niagara escarpment and the Great Pine ridge. The Great Pine ridge is the granddaddy of all glacial moraines, lying voluptuously along the north shore of Lake Ontario.

Major disturbances in the landscape are what freeway designers fret about. Freeway designers have a way of cutting and filling so that the rises and falls that used to be sharp against the horizon are now smoothed out to make it easy for cars and trucks. Where marshes used to be are now causeways with drowned, dead trees on both sides. Where escarpments used to bar the way are now long shallow cuts with high shoulders. If you accept the view of the freeway designer, then "country" is the soft-focus blur of green fields, summer fallow, distant blue silos, woodlots and exit-ramp signs that rolls endlessly back into your peripheral vision, where it is quickly erased because there are 828 kilometres of it to absorb before this trip is over.

It is difficult to pin down a memorable landscape when you are moving along the freeway at 100 km/h. Strewn with the bodies of raccoons, groundhogs and porcupines and the feathers of flickers and crows, smeared with the guts of frogs, turtles and the odd farm cat, the 401 is a constant interruption of the natural order. The 100-km/h lights of Toyotas and Freightliners confuse and wildlife comes to an abrupt end. The constant pounding of Goodyear Eagles and Michelin All-Weathers eventually reduces the creatures to a thin veneer of mortality entombed forever on the yielding asphalt.

Narrow cuts made for the freeway near Kingston give quick glimpses of laminated limestone and some rusty granite. Inadvertently there are some vistas between Shannonville and Bowmanville; but the freeway designer wants you to drive from the Quebec border to Detroit with no distractions, with just enough curves and gentle hills to keep you awake. Where there was a slope, he filled in the approach and cut through the grade so your engine wouldn't labour as you lunge through his tunnel without walls.

The speed, the gentle gradients, the spacious curves, the faithful whine of the steel-belted radials on the road, the endlessness of it all conspire to hide the life that lives beyond the next rise of land, the life at the end of the road marked by the next exit ramp. Meticulous rows of fence posts shrink one by one and disappear to their infinities as you flash by. The high blue silos are sentinels of non-urban wealth at first glance, but, on reflection, are more likely to be monsters chained invisibly to the ankles of willing but apprehensive captors – the farmers.

On your preoccupied highway trip, there is nothing to remind you of the great river – always there on the left – and the hold it has on 401-country people.

The river was there first. Great blue herons, red-winged blackbirds, perch and trout shared the clear, cold waterway for a few thousand peaceable years between the last glacier and the first Indian tribes. The Indian civilizations left hardly any monuments. Instead they endowed Niagara with an ominous spirit. They lived under the protection of another powerful Manitou among the islands in the middle reaches of the river. The Indians used the St. Lawrence and its little tributaries for open weather travel. If there was a war between tribes, the routes of supply and strategy were the rivers that nourished the great river. If it were a peaceful search for open land good for the gourds and grains they grew, then the silent canoes carried them where the water came from.

Eventually Europeans came and spoiled the neighbourhood. They were looking for short-cuts to the silks and splendours of Siam, India and China; and they came knowing there were pagan souls to save.

Le comte de Frontenac built a fort where the Cataraqui River empties into Lake Ontario because it was a busy crossroads for French traders and Indians with furs to sell. It was a good place for France to show the English that France was in the new world to stay. The French explorers, fur traders and missionaries used Cataraqui as a safe jumping-off place for their travels deeper into the interior.

Each Spring, Frontenac, Cavalier de la Salle or Dollard des Ormeaux made the trip to the Cataraqui outpost. The first, easy paddling part of their upstream journey was along the north shore of Lac St. François, past the mouths of the streams that came out of the dense bush.

Wood Creek is one of a dozen that flow south and east out of Glengarry County into Lac St. François. It is the creek closest to the Quebec border. What distinguishes it from the others? It meanders across the Condie farm. Condies have been taking pike out of Wood Creek for at least 118 years.

3   *Cash Crop Farming*

U NCLE BUD'S OLD FISH SPEAR has four barbed prongs on the end of an eight-foot ash pole as big around as the calf of your leg. Mac's spear is three-pronged with a lighter haft. Nobody can remember when spearing pike in the creek was legal, but everybody has memories of the lean fish snaking through the muddy water hunting for a safe haven that is never there – no rocks, no deep pools, no bushes to stop the running spear carriers, no place to hide from Neptune's trident as it lurches from somebody's good right hand into the shallow water. The spear is an air-to-water missile launched by a running, puffing fisherman eager for Spring's first taste of fresh-caught fish – lightly sautéed and peppered for Sunday brunch. But back when the fish and game laws were written, pike spearing became illegal and farmers found themselves poachers on their own land. The spearheads rust and the hafts gather fine grey dust in the rafters of the old drive shed over the '75 LeMans.

Andrew Condie – Mac's son, Uncle Bud's nephew – is in the barn contemplating the "new" old Massey Harris tractor. So far he has put maybe three hundred dollars worth of restoration into it. It needs a lot of work before it will be back in running order, but parts aren't that easy to come by any more. The other old Massey Harris tractor behind him is in good shape. It is 41 years old, has steel lugs instead of rubber tires, and Andrew found two new decals over in Quebec. They look pretty good on the engine hood. The Condies use this one to haul the corn augur around the barnyard.

Andrew Condie with the old Massey.

It was a raw day. First thing in the morning, light hail swirled in from the east and bounced off the slate roof of Uncle Bud's barn. Skeins of Canada geese broke through the clouds over the Adirondacks south of Lake St. Francis, joined up with others and landed in last year's corn stubble. By noon there were two thousand, with a few snows among them, resting and crooning in an almost invisible mud-coloured band stretching for three quarters of a mile south towards Bainsville.

Andrew – "nobody calls me Andy" – is the Saturday clerk at Sangster's Sons General Store in Bainsville.

'Bud' Condie and Andrew Condie.

Andrew's father, Malcolm – "everybody calls me Mac" – remembers his father taking him and his brother down to Sangster's every Spring to buy the 25-cent straw hats that were to last them all Summer. The store hasn't changed much.

Sangster's has Ultramar gas pumps out front. The big front windows have green blinds pulled most of the way down so you can read the words, Sangster's Sons General Store. On the inside wall beside the front door, the 1944 gas rationing regulations are tacked up. The Bainsville Post Office is in the left-hand corner at the back of the store, where it always was. There is a lockable swing gate that separates the post office from the store. There is a small wall of pigeon-holes – one for each family in the Bainsville area. On display in the store are rubber boots, boot liners, newspapers from Montreal, Cornwall and Alexandria, bananas, oranges, canned goods, chocolate bars, plant food, paint, miscellaneous notions. It is not the kind of retail operation anyone is going to get rich on. The real business of Sangster's is fertilizer and part of the Saturday clerk's job is to take phone orders and messages. Andrew wonders if he can keep the job at Sangster's and get another job next year over in Lancaster, looking after the lawn and garden of a lawyer's house. It wouldn't be hard. He could do the Lancaster job after five. He would take the LeMans.

Andrew has a straightforward view of his future. He is in grade eleven at Alexandria High School now. He wants to complete grade thirteen, enrol in the two-year diploma course at Kemptville College of Agricultural Technology, and then stay on the family farm. He is realistic about his chances. He knows that he's having trouble with grade eleven math.

His earliest memories of the farm are of the time when old maples lined the road from his house to Uncle Bud's house. They were so big and overgrown, their branches met over the road and formed a shadowy tunnel. Now most of them are gone and the trees that were planted to replace them haven't grown up yet.

He was kind of glad when his Uncle Bud decided to get out of the dairy business. When Andrew was young he had asthma and he couldn't stay in the barn with the cattle for too long or he would get an attack. He figures he is growing out of the asthma.

The two Condie farms are seeded to corn now. When they had cattle they could sell all the milk they could produce to different dairies in the Montreal area. There was no quota system in Quebec at the time. You could be as big and efficient as you wanted to be. Then the quota system was introduced and Uncle

Bud had to decide whether he was going to stay in the dairy business with its quotas, the deductions from the monthly milk cheque, the need to expand, rising interest rates and declining dairy product consumption. It was the identical decision faced by thousands of successful dairy farmers across Ontario during the '70s. Does a man have to start putting up with the aggravation of expanding just to make a good life for his family?

Mac Condie had a different kind of decision to make. He had moved to Montreal when he got a good job with the Sherwin Williams paint people. Then he built a bungalow about 20 rods west of the family homestead and commuted the hour's drive every day to the paint plant in Montreal. Finally, Mac decided you could take the boy out of the country but you couldn't take the country out of the boy. He left Sherwin Williams. He studied and passed the examinations to become a general insurance agent like his wife, Madge. Madge was a McIntyre from Williamstown when she married Mac. The two of them work for Rozon Insurance Brokers in Williamstown and seem to know every square foot of the Glengarry country and everybody in it.

Andrew runs in the raw wind from the barn to the drive shed.

Seventy-five years of licence plates in the Condie drive shed.

Hats for all occasions.

Tacked up on the back wall of the drive shed is a classic collection of licence plates. The oldest plate is dated 1911. Uncle Bud says he remembers the 1911 McLaughlin that his grandfather owned – the first car in the Condie family. Andrew may be having trouble with math at school but he knows his great grandfather must have kept the car around for a good long time for Uncle Bud to be able to remember it now. The McLaughlin name plate, in handsome scrolled brass, has the place of honour among the plates on the wall.

Another bright touch in the Condie drive shed is a collection of 47 colourful baseball-type caps – each one different. They advertise car dealers, implement dealers, banks, seed companies, fertilizer brands, resorts, even baseball clubs. These are the hats worn by every farmer and his sons and grandsons on every farm in the country. The hats are so popular it is practically compulsory for companies to give them away at fall fairs, ploughing matches, implement displays. Andrew decided to see how many he could collect in a Summer. Uncle Bud remarks on the number of companies that were giving away free hats one Summer and are bankrupt this year. Agribusiness was not all that buoyant through the recession.

As cash crop farmers, the Condies live in a world where daytime and nighttime temperatures determine which varieties of corn they can plant on their farms. Small talk between dairy farmers and corn growers includes much wisdom about corn heat unit ratings for the hybrids suitable for the region. The corn heat unit is a rating based on a formula that takes into account temperatures, date of the first killing fall frost, time available for field-drying the ears after the frost, moisture level of the ears for safe storage in that part of the country. The corn season in Glengarry – from planting to the first frost – is from May 18 to September 16.

Sundays the Condies go to St. Andrew's United Church, a couple of miles west on the next concession. St Andrew's sits up on the only knoll in the Lancaster flats, all by itself, surrounded by farmland. The spired church, with its graveyard, has a sparse, austere feeling to it, even in bright summer sun. You have to face the congregation when you are late for church; the pulpit backs onto the entrance.

The approach to the front door of St. Andrew's is up the narrow lane between the rows of granite gravestones. The names and dates on the stones tell of Scottish longevity in an ambiguous land that took many in infancy but let the survivors endure well beyond their 84th years. The country church keeps its dead close around to remind itself of this mortality and that immortality. The country church burying yard is the close-at-hand evidence of final destinations.

Last Saturday Mac took the LeMans over towards Williamstown "to sort of patrol" the Raisin River, to discourage anyone who might be thinking of catching fish out of season. The pickerel in Lake St. Francis swim up the Raisin, from its mouth at

Lancaster, to spawn every April. It was the kind of outdoor chore Mac liked to volunteer for, for the Lancaster Fish and Game Club. The Club and the local conservation association – with a little help from the government – were working on a scheme to save the pickerel spawning grounds.

The small talk was of fish because it was that time of year. The streams were running full. Cars by the dozen lined the service road by Lake St. Francis. Spin casters were playing man's oldest lottery for perch and pike. The trout season was a month away.

Had anyone ever tasted Lancaster perch?

The Raisin River near Williamstown, Glengarry County.

"Never heard of it."

It must be a local delicacy. Mario's Light Lunch in Lancaster has a sign out front. There's a sign on Loretta's Chip Wagon across the track. It's on the menu at the Lancaster Inn.

"Never heard of it. I'll go try it one day, if I'm hungry enough."

4　*Lancaster Perch*

C AN YOU IMAGINE? A thief broke into Loretta's Chip Wagon – through the serving window – and stole 12 pounds of fish fillets out of the fridge. Loretta's Chip Wagon! You know where it is: right there on the main street of Lancaster, north of the tracks.

If they had been run-of-the-mill frozen cod or halibut fillets, like the ones you get in boxes or polybags at the supermarket, it would have been no great loss. Frozen salt-water fish has pretty well lost all its charm by the time it gets this far inland, and you really have to gussy it up with a tartar sauce, or bread the fillets, or bake them in some sort of heavy-duty marinade, to replace the fresh-fish taste that's lost in the freezing.

But these were perch fillets – freshly caught perch fillets from Lake St. Francis – caught, skinned and gutted and put in the fridge by Maurice Derouchie on the morning of the day they were stolen. There is nothing fresher than that, mister.

Maurice is Loretta's husband.

At $4.99 a pound, retail, that was a nickel short of a $60 heist. Whoever did it must have assumed the Derouchies were sound sleepers and would not hear the noise of a rupturing window frame in the middle of the night, because the Derouchie house – next to the chip wagon – is on the side opposite to the serving window. You'd think a dog would have barked or someone would have heard something; but the thief assumed correctly and he got clean away with it. The $60 represented about $175 worth of lost business that day, when you figure the Derouchies' mark-up and the Pepsis and fries that people would have bought.

The thief must have known what practically everybody along the river knows: fillets from fresh-caught perch, briefly sautéed in a little butter, have the delicious, nutty flavour of fresh-water fish and a definite taste of their own. It's the taste you dream of when you go into a seafood specialty restaurant; but no matter how hard the restaurant tries, the taste is muted, elusive – just a faint allusion to what it might have been.

Not everyone knows where to go to get properly cooked Lancaster perch. The Lancaster Inn down on old number two makes a big deal out of the local specialty. You can sit in their dining room and look out over the Lake where the fish are caught and pay $7.95 for four or five fillets deep-fried in heavy batter. The only way a serious fish eater can get even part of his money's worth is to peel off the layer of batter, set it aside, and concentrate on the naked perch. Lancaster perch is so good it can survive this kind of mistreatment from the well-meaning cook.

On the other hand, Loretta is in the fast-food, limited-menu, roadside marketing business. She hasn't got time to ruin the fish by overcooking it in a greasy batter. She sautées and peppers it lightly and quickly. Served with decent french fries and cole slaw at $4.65 a plate, the perch's fresh distinctive taste is addictive. It doesn't need the traditional lemon wedge that most restaurants serve with fish, to cut through the grease and batter that smothered its subtle taste during the cooking.

The thing of it is, Loretta's perch was caught that morning – six hours ago, to be exact – by Maurice. He was up and on his way to the dock in his black and silver pick-up before seven

Loretta Derouchie.

o'clock. Maurice parks the pick-up close to the door of his one-boat boat house beside the dock at Lancaster South. He gets out the bait bucket of silvery minnows. He stores what he needs aboard the 16-foot skiff. The little outboard motor pushes him out to where he knows the perch are.

This morning Maurice's boat is a small dot at the far side of Lake St. Francis, close to the St. Lawrence Seaway channel. From this distance he looks no bigger than one of the channel buoys. A huge black ship, the *Algoport* – downbound between the Snell and the Beauharnois – rides high in the water. Maurice's boat rocks in her wake.

When he comes back to South Lancaster, just before noon, Maurice notices the three retired clothing merchants from Montreal. They are lined up like aging seagulls on the dock. Their rods are at a 45-degree angle. Their lard pails are beside the aluminum chairs, ready to receive the day's catch. The comfortable exchange of familiar jokes and insults helps the time to pass.

Maurice runs the boat into the boat house and hauls the nose up out of the water. He sits on a low box and sets to work beheading, skinning and gutting the morning's catch. He tosses the fillets into a pail of ice water. In a few minutes there will be from 12 to 20 pounds of fillets ready for the day's business at Loretta's Chip Wagon.

Maurice Derouchie.

As a matter of fact it isn't a chip wagon at all. It's a 1969 Chevrolet C-50 bus with a neat stainless steel galley where the passengers used to sit. There's barely room for three people in the narrow space between the serving window and the grill.

Business is good. Travelling salesmen park their LeBarons beside the bus and straighten out their order books while they eat the $4.65 plate. A provincial police constable stops for his lunch.

Teenagers order the $1.85 fish roll and a Pepsi. The fish roll is a couple of fillets on a hot-dog roll.

Is the perch that good? Or is it the daydream of the case-hardened traveller whose salivary glands – jaded by too many pretentious expense-account meals at Winston's and Fenton's – cry out for the subtle perfection of taste that someday will emerge, romantically, from the most unlikely of all kitchens: the spartan lunch counter in the hard-to-reach location that's worth driving miles out of your way to enjoy?

It is that good.

Loretta and Maurice do not dream of a chain of converted Chevy busses along the shore of the St. Lawrence. They doubt that a multinational food conglomerate is going to open a franchise chain of Loretta's Chip Wagons and run lifestyle commercials on television to build customer traffic. There is only one Lake St. Francis, only one Maurice, only one Loretta, only one converted bus north of the tracks in Lancaster. This is what they mean when they say "small is beautiful."

5   *Big Is Bountiful*

"Y OU SEE in the olden days the young women of a farmer's household did most of the milking and a milking hour lover was sure to be doubly welcome," writes an unknown country author. "He could help milk and also come in handy in carrying the brimming pails to the dairy or milkhouse."

But where is the three-legged stool? Where is the straw-hatted farmer's daughter who crouched on it with a shiny pail between her knees? Where is the barn cat at which one could squirt the wet and welcome missile of milk? Where is the strainer pail with its fine steel mesh in the pouring spout? Where are the milk cans? Where is the separator room? Where are the tie stalls and the mangers full of last Summer's timothy and alfalfa, pushed down through a trapdoor in the barn floor from the haymow above?

Times have changed.

The Grant farm – at Grant's Corners on the Boundary Road – is just beyond the city limits of Cornwall. Rod Grant's childhood, adolescence and maturity all happened during the years of the Beatles, television's golden age, the rise of the computer, the agribusiness revolution. It didn't hurt a bit.

Rod Grant is one of the "& Sons" of Millard Grant & Sons, dairy farmers. Millard and sons Barry and Rod farm more than a thousand acres to feed their herd of Holstein cattle, which includes 185 cows that have to be milked twice a day, seven days a week, 52 weeks a year.

At milking time, the 185 black and white cows are in their usual holding pattern in the long barn behind the sterilized steel and concrete milking parlour. Their great-veined udders strain with the weight of their milk. Some dribbles to the floor as they wait their turn in the milking parlour. This is no Noah's Ark, where the animals came in two by two. These cows come in 12 by 12. The barrier lifts, the two doors open. On each side, 12 cows file in on the steel-grated, raised floor. They angle-park them-

Twenty-four at a time in the milking parlour, Grants' farm, Stormont County.

selves hip to hip with their gaunt behinds aimed at the sunken centre aisle. When the doors close, stanchions hold the cows firmly in position. They are used to it, like passengers in the economy section of a jumbo jet.

Like a rubber-booted flight attendant, a man walks up and down the aisle between the two rows of cows and gives the udder and hindquarters of each cow a generous splashing of disinfectant. Rod and one of the neighbour's boys come along quickly behind and attach the suction gear to the teats. A flexible and sterilized pipeline goes from the suction cups on the cow's udder, through a metering device, to a stainless steel piping system that carries the whole milk into the storage tank in the next room.

The metering device measures the rate of flow of milk. When that drops off, the suction action is stopped, the suction equipment releases the teats and the unit automatically lifts up and to the side – out of the way of the cow. Then each teat is dipped in a disinfectant that also has the effect of shrinking the size of the aperture so that infections cannot travel up into the cow's lactation system. She is now ready to walk, lock-step with her sisters, out of the milking parlour, into a U-turn that takes them back to the barn where they can roam loose and are free to eat, digest and doze until it is time to be milked again.

At no time in the milking process has the milk been in contact with the outside world. On its way to the stainless steel storage tank it went through a heat transfer system where the heat in the milk was released and used to add heat to the hot water system.

As the first 24 cows leave, the next 24 arrive at the other end. The process is repeated until all 185 are done. Rod uses the time in the parlour to inspect each cow carefully. He looks for signs of infection or improvement in an animal that is under treatment for a minor ailment. He carefully checks the cows in their lactation. He examines the old reliables to see if there are signs they should be replaced.

There follows a thorough spraying down of the milking parlour with hot water and disinfectant. The stainless steel pipeline system is flushed out twice in hot water, once with a disinfecting detergent rinse, the second time with a mild acid solution. Now the parlour is ready for the next milking. The big tank is half full of cool milk.

Disinfecting cow's udder before attaching suction cups; Grants' farm, Stormont County.

Next day – and every day – at noon the Villeneuve Transport truck from Moose Creek arrives and takes more than nine tons or 7,400 quarts of whole milk from the full storage tank, then hauls it to Kraft Foods Limited in Ingleside (one of the "new" towns created when the St. Lawrence Seaway was built). The Grants pay extra transportation charges for this daily service.

It is unusual for a dairy farm to ship milk every day as the Grants do. In the 1981 census there were 17,630 dairy farms in Ontario. Most of these farms were about a third the size of the Grants', with from 45 to 65 milking cows. Only 374 of them had 90 milking cows or more. The Grant farm is big.

The dairy parlour that processes 24 cows at a time on its two raised floors is designed to reduce labour to a minimum. There is no more squatting, squeezing, lifting, pouring or straining. These 185 cows can be milked by two people in less than three hours. Two people with the fastest hands in the West would be able to milk only 25 cows by hand in three hours. Over the years Holsteins have been cross bred to achieve an animal with a voracious appetite, an efficient lactation system, strong legs, and a docile temperament. Heifers and semen from desirable blood lines are expensive. Holstein breeders can take 20 to 30 years to get their herds into optimum condition. The Grant herd is a

Nine tons of milk every day go to Ingleside.

commercial herd. Its blood lines were selected over the years for a reasonable level of protein conversion and for a trouble-free, healthy life cycle – the ideal for a big-volume dairy farm.

Feeding the cows enough of the right kind of food at the right price increases the volume of milk each cow can produce. The menu here includes whole-plant silage, haylage, cob and kernel silage, soy bran, mineral supplements and water. Holsteins are remarkable converters of vegetable protein into milk. When each cow is eating the right proportions of the menu her milk production is high.

Cattle don't graze much any more. They stay indoors all Fall, Winter and Spring. They are let out for a few hours each day during the Summer but spend most of their lives indoors in barn-sized pens. As farmers work to keep unit costs down by enlarging their scale of operations, this country that seems to have an endless supply of space moves closer each year to the "zero grazing units" of the Japanese, who have no space at all – farms

Silos store whole-plant silage, haylage, cob and kernel silage.

where the cattle never leave the barn except when they go to the slaughter house.

Growing the feed for a herd this size is a major production. All the farm implements are on a gigantic scale because a lot of corn has to be planted in the short planting season; a lot of corn has to be harvested in the short harvesting season; a lot of hay has to be harvested during the best of summer days, to fill the silos and keep the cows well fed through the Winter. Rocks have to be picked each Spring before planting. Rod jokes that the Grants are sometimes a day or two later than their neighbours getting the corn in because they have such a huge rock harvest to do first.

"Picking rocks is not a great intellectual challenge. Put your mind in neutral," Rod tells a group of high-school students. They are hired to harvest the glacial pebbles that break through the deep till to the surface every Spring.

In the days when cattle were in tie stalls and had a layer of straw bedding, cleaning the stables was the most demeaning job on the farm. You forked the manure into the litter carrier, pushed the carrier out the stable door and dumped it on the manure pile. In the Spring you forked it all into the manure spreader. The spreader shredded and flung the manure across the field like crazy brown confetti.

Then the automatic stable cleaner and the front end loader came along and took some of the backache out of the dirty chore. And today there is a low concrete holding tank behind the silos.

"The four silos dominate the gentle Stormont countryside"; Grants' farm.

The holding tank gets a daily contribution of the cattle's excretions. Once in the Fall and once in the Spring, before planting, the contents of the tank are agitated and pumped into a liquid manure spreader which recycles the nutrients taken out of the field last season in the form of hay and corn. The circle is complete: from the field to the silo to the cow to the holding tank to the field.

The four silos dominate the gentle Stormont countryside. They loom over the daily life of the farm too because they must be filled with the right mixture of nourishment, proteins and bulk so that 185 cows will produce nine tons of whole milk every day. They must be filled in time to empty as next year's hay harvest begins.

Tall silos and low barns, a two-story red brick Victorian house from the nineteenth century close by, a new ranch bungalow on its own well-kept lot next door – these identify the new agriculture in 401 country. Farms have to be big enough to grow food economically. One man alone cannot manage to do all the

The next generation of Grants going to school.

work of cultivating, fertilizing, spraying, seeding, harvesting, silo-filling, milking, feeding, watering, cleaning. Partnerships are the natural evolution of the traditional family farm.

A farmer used to work 100 acres until he died and passed it on to his middle-aged son who repeated the process. Now, with mega-farms, the father and sons create a corporate partnership, keep the land and the homestead in the family and expand as they must to produce at competitive prices.

The Grants have such a partnership. Millard and Norma Grant live in the new ranch bungalow on the corner. Their son Barry and his wife and five children live on the Grant homestead. Rod and his wife and four children are in the farmhouse on another farm about an eighth of a mile away.

"We're close enough for consultation; but not so close we get on each other's nerves."

Lean and fit at 73, Millard Grant contributes his wisdom, maintenance and part-time labour to the partnership. Barry and Rod share the principal responsibilities and spell each other off for holidays. Each gets every other Sunday off.

It was a rainy, foggy morning late in May. The humidity intensified the pungent milk smell and the piercing ammonia fumes of the manure.

"Day like this makes you want to have more fans in the barn."

None of the Grants apologizes for bigness. "There are more plusses than minuses in what we have here. Yes, we're big because milk is a big business. I guess we have a bigger equity in something than some of our friends from school are able to put together. They tease us about that. We just tease back about banker's hours and long holiday weekends."

"We're self-employed. I think that's important."

"Our wives get involved. Our children get involved. That's harder to do when you've got an office job in the city."

"Marriages last longer in the country. The odds seem to be better that couples are going to stay on an even keel. I think the kids in the country see more of their parents than some kids in the city. Out here we seem to be able to do a lot of things together on the farm. We get involved in what each of us is doing. I think it's because our dad brought us into things when we were kids. He had a way, he still has a way of making things interesting. I think that's it."

The bigness is softened around the farmyard by the bikes and toys and unfinished projects of the Grant grandchildren. The Dion wagons are lined up in the yard. One of the 11 tractors had its engine lifted out for a major overhaul.

Venerable and foreign, an old Renault N70 and a red Nuffeld tractor look like little visitors from another planet beside the high and mighty White Field Boss, Case AgriKing and the Allis Chalmers 7000.

"We're not all that sold on the big four-wheel drives. They might get you out on the land earlier in the spring, but they sure pack it down. You have to think about soil structure, especially when you use a fair amount of commercial fertilizer."

Over in Leeds County on highway 42, Harry Van Bruggen tells another story about dairy farming. Harry's mother and father came to Leeds County with their seven children from Holland after World War II.

"A good decision, yes. My father wanted a dairy farm. We were farming 350 acres until 1967. This is not the worst land for farming. It's well drained, except for that patch down behind the barn. It floods in the Spring, but we could always get a crop of buckwheat off it."

"We'd done well all those years, but the quota system got us down. As soon as I could I switched to clocks. Repairing them. It was something I picked up. And I like repairing them, putting them back in action. It was a risk, but it meant money coming in for something I liked doing."

"Everybody in the country tries to get more than one source of income. Hairdressing. Renting construction equipment. Book-keeping. Bees."

Instead of salt and pepper shakers, creamers and vinegar cruets, Harry's kitchen table is covered with his delicate clock-repairing tools. There are clocks all around him: mantel clocks, clocks in marble and mahogany, art deco models, clocks without hands, clocks without faces, weight-driven clocks, wind-ups and electrics, even old tin alarm clocks – all patients in The Clock Hospital, R.R.1, Delta, Ontario.

Harry Van Bruggen's customers come from Quebec, southern Ontario, northern New York. Antique dealers bring him mortally wounded clocks to fix for the big auction sale. He always gives a six-month guarantee.

"Word of mouth has done it. People tell people."

From behind a kitchen chair, Harry lifts out an American clock movement, made – save for two small parts – entirely of hardwood. It is 185 years old. He holds it up and thumbs the wooden gears that still make that satisfying meshing sound. One day when he is in the mood he's going to place it inside a handsome pillared mantel clock and get it running again.

Heidi Oeggerli put cowbells on the necks of a few heifers to remind her of home.

"And the neighbours like the sound of it."

Until 1969, home for Paul and Heidi Oeggerli was Switzerland. They were farming 15 acres of land. Both had attended agricultural college and they were committed to farming; but there didn't seem to be much of a future for the children because there was no land for sale. Farming is different in Switzerland. In the

Heidi Oeggerli of Heidi Farms, Glengarry County.

late '60s, a friend visiting from Quebec suggested they think about Canada.

Paul came first, in 1969, and got a job as a hired hand on a Jersey dairy farm near Paris, Ontario. Heidi came a little later with the children. For two years they put in long hours, spent no money, and travelled western Ontario looking at farms for sale – farms they couldn't afford; but they expected that the day would come when they would find what they wanted.

In 1971 they realized that western Ontario was too expensive for them so they travelled into eastern Ontario and discovered what they were after in Glengarry County – across the road from St. Andrew's United Church. It was a medium-sized dairy farm with a quota, and a house that could use a little fixing up. The owner wanted $25,000 as a down payment. The Oeggerlis had saved $20,000. They went to see the Toronto-Dominion bank manager in Paris. He knew them. He had watched them accumulate the $20,000. The T-D loaned the Oeggerlis another $10,000.

They paid the $25,000 down and had $5,000 for fertilizer and seed corn. For the past 14 years they have been building up their line of credit, buying or renting extra milk quota as soon as they could, acquiring more land whenever they could afford it.

Home is now Heidi Farms in Glengarry – a picture-postcard farm with its red barn, high silos, white house, fruit trees, Mugho pines – and the heifers with the Alpine bells stick their heads over the white fence and watch Heidi cutting the lawn with the riding mower.

Feeding the cattle in the Oeggerli dairy barn is a different scene from the Grants'. The 125 cows are loose in big pens and have their choice at any time of haylage or whole plant silage or protein and mineral supplement.

The supplement is responsible for a significant increase in milk production, so the Oeggerlis put in a computerized feeding system that tells them on a print-out every morning which cows are eating enough supplement and which cows are "off their feed" and not producing as much milk.

Each cow takes her turn eating the supplement at one of the six feeding stalls in the barn. Each cow wears a "transponder" around her neck. The transponder sends an electronic signal that identifies her as she steps into the feeding stall.

The feeding stall has a sensor that picks up the cow's identification. The sensor passes this along to the computer which then tells the storage tank to release the appropriate ration of protein supplement.

Every morning Paul's son, young Paul, can press the print button and pull a print-out that shows him how much supplement each cow ate during the last 24 hours. The system quickly pinpoints the cow that is off her feed and lets father and son correct the problem before it can grow into a crisis.

One of Paul Oeggerli's Holsteins wearing the transponder that signals the computerized feeding system to release her ration of proteins for the day; Glengarry County.

Young Paul graduated from the diploma course at Kemptville College of Agricultural Technology so he is deeply involved with his father in the management and improvement of the herd.

Breeding for the future used to be a clumsy affair on the dairy farm. Farmers kept an eye on the cows, watching for signs that it was mating time. The big-shouldered bull with the ring in its nose had to be trotted out to meet the physiological needs of the cow – a need that lasts for only a few hours.

Times have changed.

The bull with the ring in its nose is gone, replaced by an ampule of semen that arrives in a syringe in a portable deep-freeze. When the cow signals she is ready – mounting, or being mounted by, other cows for example – big daddy is taken out of the deep freeze and administered manually.

When artificial insemination was introduced, experts provided the service. A farmer who wanted his cows to be fathered by a particular sire bought the entire insemination process from the owner of the bull. Now farmers have learned to administer the semen themselves. They have a wider choice of sires.

Paul and his brother Walter, who is at Kemptville now, are the wave of the future: young, well-educated in the Glengarry tradition, working beside a professional and committed father in the complex world of agribusiness.

6   Turtle in the Rainbarrel

ONE OF THE CRITES BOYS was over on Wales Island the other day and heard high-pitched squawking in the bushes under the big pines. It was an angry and forlorn ball of yellowish fluff – about the size of a cantaloupe melon – tottering around in the dry leaves. Deprived, God knows how, of its security in its nest on the pine branch, the baby great-horned owl was not a willing captive. He pecked savagely at young Crites, who decided he would have to take the helpless infant home to Long Sault. There was no sign of the nest, nor of a concerned adult bird. He could either leave it there and hope the mother will find it, or he could take it home, maybe feed it until it grows up and flies away.

Mrs. Crites doesn't know what to do with a *yak-yak-yak*ing little creature with a menacing beak and oversized, angry eyes. She doesn't know what owls feed their young. She phones Bryce Rupert at the bird sanctuary. He ought to know. Besides, he's probably a distant relative and that's what relatives are for.

Bryce doesn't think it's a good idea to take in the owl chick. But Don Gillap, the resource technician at the sanctuary, jumps into the pick-up anyway, goes over to Long Sault and brings the owl chick back in a small aluminum cage. He stops at Ingleside on the way for a pound of ground beef.

The owl yaks and pecks at the cage. Bryce looks at it, bemused

Monogamous geese are fiercely protective of their goslings. Ducks and drakes may be a little stupid about their ducklings on dry land, but they at least stay close to them. In any case, the Upper Canada Migratory Bird Sanctuary is not exactly an orphanage for every waif or stray that comes along.

One of them – Bryce or Don – has the bright idea of phoning the "bird lady" over in Verona, the one that runs the bird hospital. She writes a column in the *Whig Standard* Saturdays. She'll know what to do.

The bird lady isn't too impressed when she hears about it; but one of her volunteer "flying angels" from Cornwall turns up the next day and takes the baby owl over to Verona. Bryce says he must remember to tell the Crites what's happening.

It is a burgeoning Sunday afternoon in Spring. It is difficult not to think about the Indian blood that runs, diluted, in Bryce Rupert's veins. (His Loyalist roots date back to 1784 when Peter Rupert arrived in Osnabruck Township with his full-blooded Mohawk wife, Catherine Littlefawn.) He sees where the Virginia white-tail deer have nibbled off the tender top growth of new aspen seedlings. He notes where hundred-year-old fence lines were on Frank Fogarty's farm, which is now overgrown with ironwood and poplar by the river. Like a self-trained archaeologist, Bryce reconstructs the life of the sugar bush from fragments of sap pails, angle iron, square-headed nails, hand-hewn logs – all that's left now of a sugar-making cabin that may have been used last in the '30s.

When he comes to an open glade in the bush, he wiggles all his fingers to demonstrate how the worms ate the heart out of a maple tree until it rotted and finally toppled to make the space where vines, poplars and ironwoods now have enough sun to flourish.

The same expressive fingers mimic the wood ducklings, illustrating how their tiny toenails allow them to climb up and out of the nests in the deep holes that had been drilled by pileated woodpeckers in a dead maple trunk.

Kids come to the sanctuary in Scout troops and Sunday school classes. Bryce Rupert takes them out to the nature trails – usually to the bee tree – and tells them to put their ears to the trunk so they can hear the humming of the swarm 20 feet above their heads. To test the gullible, he tells them honey will pour from the tree if he drills a hole in it.

The sanctuary's 6,400 acres include Upper Canada Village, Crysler Farm Park, the golf course, the marina, the campgrounds and a corner of Lake St. Lawrence. It is the northern nesting home for about two thousand Canada geese who winter in the mouth of the Delaware river, on Chesapeake Bay, in the Carolinas and Florida. During the Fall feeding time, about 30,000 visiting geese use the sanctuary as a pit stop en route to the Chesapeake. The great Atlantic flyway is to the east of Upper Canada and the Mississippi flyway is far to the west. The reason so many geese ignore the main flyways is that naturalists borrowed some Canada geese raised in captivity in Delaware and built suitable nesting sites for them; the new young geese naturally came back every Spring, bringing Maryland and Virginia friends with them.

Upper Canada Migratory Bird Sanctuary, northern nesting grounds for 2,000 Canada geese.

The neighbourhood is changing. Five years ago cormorants started to nest in the sanctuary. Black-backed gulls, brown threshers and cuckoos are some of the new birds among the 150-plus species that have been identified here.

Most of the human visitors are from Montreal, Ottawa, Kingston and Toronto. Field naturalists, birders, television commentators, photographers, overstressed businessmen come to the sanctuary for an afternoon, a day, a week or three weeks. Most come to fish the St. Lawrence. First to arrive in April are the "garbage" fishermen – aficionados who are not snobbish about what they catch and eat. Heaven for them is when they can fill a pail with mudpout – a fish of prehistoric ugliness with whiskers on each side of its mouth. Also known as catfish or *barbotte*, they are sweet tasting but must be caught before the St. Lawrence warms up. Downstream in Lake St. Francis, perch proliferate. Up and down the river, pike, 'lunge, bass, brown and rainbow trout and pickerel thrive enough to keep the campgrounds filled to 75% capacity.

In the Summer, 1,000 geese and 2,000 ducks are banded at the sanctuary. When adult geese have lost some of their flight feathers and the goslings are not mature enough to fly, the naturalists will round the geese up, using a length of snow-fence and a couple of pickets. The ducks – blacks, mallards, wood ducks, pintails, teals and widgeon – are lured to a big rectangular screen trap in the middle of the main pond.

General factotum, curator and P.R. expert in this haven for migratory exiles is Loyalist Bryce Rupert. He jumps into the

Mazda pick-up and goes for cedar to repair the picnic tables. Then he drives down the abandoned roadbed of the Great Northern Railway to check the downstream water control gates that maintain the level of water in the lagoons and swamps of the sanctuary. When Hydro tells the St. Lawrence Seaway Parks Commission that it is planning to raise the level of the river – something to do with the Saunders generating station at Cornwall – Bryce can insert logs into the upstream and downstream control gates to keep the sanctuary's own water levels constant.

Bryce Rupert, Upper Canada Migratory Bird Sanctuary.

This way, the nests of geese, ducks and waders are protected.

He kicks the body of a dead carp into the water so the gulls will come along and scavenge it. He stops beside a pond where there are two long tree trunks half submerged. It is a favourite place for turtles to sun themselves because it is away from the well-travelled trails. He pulls out the field glasses he keeps on the shelf in the Mazda.

"Oldtimers used to keep a turtle in their rainbarrel as a kind of weather forecaster. They'd put a piece of firewood in the rainbarrel. If the weather was going to be sunny the turtle would sit on the piece of floating wood. If the weather was going to be bad, the turtle would slide off the wood and stay in the water. That's what I was told," Bryce says. He aims the field glasses at the long black logs, but there are no turtles to be seen.

Life is not easy for a turtle. It begins in a clutch of eggs laid in a sandy or gravelly place near a swamp. The old Great Northern roadbed is ideal. Having laid her eggs, the turtle abandons them to the heat of the sun for three months of incubation. If the eggs have not been eaten by skunks, porcupines, muskrats, herons or gulls, the baby turtles – self-reliant the instant they crawl out of their shells – head for the swamp. A moving target is slightly safer than one buried in shallow gravel. If they reach the swamp alive, they forage for food along the edge and in the water. To swallow the food they must keep their heads under water.

Predator animals like to hunt in swamps and on the edge of ponds; but the turtle has a curious defence mechanism: it is an air-breather – with lungs like us – but it can also extract oxygen from water through gills in its throat and another set of gills in its anus. It can stay under water almost indefinitely when predators lie in wait on the shore.

The spotted turtle *(Clemmys guttata)* is on the list of endangered species. It has been driven to near-extinction because man drains and fills the swamps and ponds that were once its natural habitat. You may find a spotted turtle in one small region of Ontario bisected by the 401; but the only way to save it now may be in the captivity of a zoo.

It is a time of meditation for the turtles in the sanctuary. When the sun is warm they will line up on the half-submerged log and blink a little. They have survived. They are now too big for the great blue heron's beak. They can plop forward into the water in a nanosecond and evade the clumsy skunk. The sun is warm. The bird-watchers and naturalists are no trouble. They keep their distance. Next Spring one of the lady turtles will swim and crawl across to the bank of the old railway line, wiggle and kick backwards into the gravel to dig a hole and eventually leave a clutch of eggs to the whim of an ambiguous Nature.

It turns out that Bryce Rupert is the turtles' keeper. There is hope.

7   The Lockmaster

W HEN LOCKMASTER BOB BURGESS comes on the "A" shift
Friday morning at eight o'clock one of Paterson's lakers,
the *Quedoc*, has her nose on the upper fender and is ready to be
locked through. Two of the linesmen, Allan Bailey and Cal Elliott,
are all ready beside the empty lock, where they will haul down
the two cables from the aft deck. The first really warming sun
of the year is welcome on their backs. The air is clear and clean.
Last night's rain was good for the grass.

Bailey is thinking about buying a new camera. It isn't an easy
decision because he already owns a video camera and a cheap
35-millimetre that takes pretty good pictures. His wife isn't too
impressed with the idea. All the same, it's nice to think about
a solid 35-millimetre with a 26-105 zoom lens. That would be
all you'd need. Maybe a Minolta.

Cal Elliott is thinking about weekends. He likes his weekends.
He's lucky. He was taken on at the Seaway a couple of months
ago and has just qualified as a linesman. If it turns out the job
is permanent, he can plan. He came to Upper Canada with his
folks from Lowesport, Newfoundland. His father teaches over at
the Seafarers' Institute at Morrisburg. Cal has knocked around
a bit. He worked around the yachts at Ontario Place and down
in Florida. He has shipped out as a deckhand and wheelman on
the lakeboats.

"Really didn't like that. I missed Friday nights off the most."

The *Quedoc* eases into the lock and the linesmen chat with
her deckhands as she slides by. The linesmen and the deckhands
look as though they aren't really paying attention, as though
they don't have to. They've done it so many times before. But
the deck officer pays attention. He murmurs into his walkie-
talkie as he paces back and forth, peering over the side to judge
the distance from the side of the lock to the hull, and the speed
of the ship. And lockmaster Burgess pays attention. He walks
beside the ship and calls out the distances to the ship's captain
through his amplified walkie-talkie.

The off-handedness of the linesmen and deckhands is a pose.
The cables slide through the fairleads at the right moment. The
loops slip over the bollards. The winches whine. Everything happens on schedule, as it should.

It is not the busiest of shifts. The *Vandoc* comes down. The
Doan Transport goes up. *Salt Spray* – an Aloha yacht based in
Ottawa – is the first pleasure craft of the day. She is locked
throughout without having to tie up alongside. Allan Bailey
swings over to *Salt Spray* an aluminum pole with a clipboard

welded to the end. The skipper of *Salt Spray* clips a $5 bill to it and they are on their way. A Seaway workboat goes through and ties up downstream. *Notre Dame de Rosaire* – a "salty" from Manila – goes through with a short Filipino captain and a tall American pilot side by side on the rusty flying bridge. *Sheila Yeates* – a two-masted schooner from Duluth – comes downstream. Her lean, tanned, silver-haired captain stands high in the cockpit with one foot on the wheel. A svelte young woman in a pink bikini is spread-eagled on the fore deck. The other four crew members wear cashmere sweaters and new topsiders.

"We're headed for Quebec City, the Gaspé, St. Anthony's in Newfoundland and the Labrador," the captain calls up. "How far is it to Eisenhower?"

Free of the lock, the *Sheila Yeates* sets a square lateen sail and runs ahead of the wind towards the Eisenhower Lock 26 miles downstream.

Between ships, the conversation drifts from cameras to the union vote, to the good life on shore in Iroquois, a town of 1,200 house-proud souls, to life at sea in an even more confined community.

Lockmaster Burgess is a camera bug too. He and linesman Bailey carry on informal photography seminars when there is time. Burgess fetches his nylon tote bag with the Nikon and the 24-millimetre lens from his pick-up so he can show Bailey what he means.

When no ships are expected, the lockmaster takes a long inspection tour. He goes down to the control tower for a brief chat with Dwayne Gow, the lock motorman. Then he climbs down a circular steel ladder underground beside the lock to inspect the electric motors that open and close the heavy sector gates. He walks the full length of the tunnel beside the lock to the tower at the upstream end where a student linesman is scrubbing the floor. He glances across the lock at the viewing terrace. There are two sight-seeing busses.

"Isn't it strange? Tour busses can always manage to arrive between ships."

Under the hot afternoon sun, he looks at the fenders where the ships rub their bows as they line up to enter the lock. The fenders are 12-inch by 12-inch white oak timbers 12 feet long, bolted three deep to the side of the tie wall. The friction of the steel hulls frays the oak until it hangs like a long tattered dish rag. Sometimes the friction is so furious the wood catches fire and smoulders for days without creating any visible smoke. When the timbers are frayed and useless they are replaced. The old ones sometimes go to the employees of the Seaway, who use them for walkways and retaining walls for gardens at home.

The men along the Seaway belong to the Canadian Brotherhood of Railway Transport and General Workers Union. A ballot box has been set up for them in a back office in the lockmaster's building. The members are voting on whether to change from eight-hour shifts to twelve-hour shifts. Every other local has opted for the twelve-hour shift. The gossip around Iroquois is that the younger members like the idea of the twelve-hour shift because it gives them long, uninterrupted weekends with their families. Older members prefer to stay with the eight-hour shift because they're set in their ways after so many years of annual rotation from shift to shift. One of the senior people is planning to vote against the twelve-hour shift because his arthritis really acts up after eight hours on the job; but he doesn't tell anybody his reason.

Bob Burgess hands over at four that afternoon. He packs his camera gear into the pick-up and goes home to Island Park Drive. Linesman Allan Bailey moves into the lockmaster's office and is acting lockmaster for "B" shift. He is taking the place of the regular lockmaster who is on leave that day. Nine years at the Iroquois lock have qualified Bailey for the job.

"B" shift is a busy eight hours. The *Canadian Ranger* and Miseners' *J.N. McWatter* are locked through downbound. Both are 222 metres long, the longest and widest ships that can fit in the Seaway locks. Their stems are talked down to the "Y" position, which is only 16 feet from the safety cable. There is no margin for error.

The *Athol*, registered in Monrovia, goes upstream, with Orientals handling the deck winches and an Occidental deck officer wielding his walkie-talkie like a cowboy's revolver in a western movie. Acting lockmaster Bailey has his walkie-talkie strapped discreetly under his jacket and he brings the fist-sized microphone to his chin as if he were talking to someone hidden up his right sleeve.

The *Elmglen* is loaded to Seaway depth with Durham wheat. One of the deckhands poses in the slanting evening light with his guitar and plays a few heavy chords to an old rock lyric. Two more deckhands play a solemn game of catch with a baseball that bounces wildly on the metal deck and rolls hundreds of feet past its target.

The new moon is in its proper place above the row of Lombardy poplars. The floodlights along the lock show the yellow markers painted on the concrete to subdivide the distance between the upper gate and the lower gate. The *Algoport* – all $30,000,000 worth of her – is riding high in the water because

Linesman and lockmaster "talk" ship towards lower end of Eisenhower Lock, Massena, New York.

she is light and downbound for Montreal and Cape Breton. She is 201 metres long. The lock is 233.5 metres long. No time to be casual, but, then, ships' captains and lockmasters are never casual.

The *Algoport*'s riding lights and superstructure lights come into view as she rounds Galop Island.

The lockmaster, alone in his office at the centre-line of the lock, picks up the phone and tells the Seaway control tower in

St. Lambert that the *Algoport* is approaching the Iroquois lock. The lock motorman, alone in the control tower at the lower end of the Iroquois lock, hears the lockmaster's report. The linesmen, at the upper end of the lock, hear it too. Everyone has been expecting the *Algoport* at about this time of night. The traffic sheet at the start of "B" shift indicated she was between Gananoque and Brockville.

Clear and weightless voices in the night, from the ship to St. Lambert, from St. Lambert to Iroquois, and back again, pass the mammoth ore-carrier from one to another down the river. The lockmaster, the lock motorman, the linesmen all hear the *Algoport* change from the Canadian radio frequency to the American frequency at Crossover Island. Depending on the pilot on the *Algoport*, and if she's riding light, you can estimate her arrival at Iroquois fairly accurately.

As she approaches the lock, her bow becomes a black mass, blacker than the night, slowly obliterating the floodlights one by one, cutting off the view of the moon over the poplar trees.

The lockmaster takes a clipboard off its hook and checks the length of the *Algoport* one more time. Then he straps the radio transmitter to his hip, puts on his midnight-blue windbreaker and goes out to meet the ship.

The voice of the lockmaster is amplified and can be heard for nearly a mile along the approaches to the lock. It is an authoritative, one-sided conversation he carries on with the ship's captain. His calm, I-know-what-I'm-doing voice rings out of the invisible speakers along the channel. It is his lock and he is in charge. There are no options once the entry manoeuvre begins.

This night, because he is riding light and there is a steady wind, the captain of *Algoport* chooses to run the nose of the ship along the fender wall leading to the lock. With the bow touching the wall and the stern riding a few metres out from the wall, the long hull is held parallel to the lock. When the bow reaches the upper gate, the ship is in perfect relationship to the lock and enters with only a few metres to spare on either side. The engines are at slow speed. The implicit momentum, the steady throbbing of far-off diesels, the moving wall of black-painted steel beside him tell the lockmaster something about the captain, something about how the captain responds to the massive tonnage under his feet.

"*Algoport*, stop at the lower ten-metre mark, the lower ten-metre mark."

The ten-metre mark is 15 metres this side of the colossal safety cable stretched across the lock. The cable is strong enough to stop a full-loaded ship that enters the lock at too high a speed.

Without the cable, even a slow-moving ship could plough into the lock gates and close the entire Seaway from the head of the lakes to the Atlantic Ocean. Captains, their Seaway pilots and the lockmaster are not impressed if a ship stops within three metres of the cable.

"Twenty-five metres. Twenty-five."

The lockmaster slowly paces along beside the high snub-nosed stem. He calls out the distance from the forward tip of the ship to the ten-metre mark. Softly, in the background, another voice, not amplified, is telling the captain where the stem of the ship is. It is the voice of a deck officer on his walkie-talkie, telling

"Three metres three." "One metre one." "In position." "Close the upper end."

his wheelman where *Algoport* is in the lock, but he is standing at least ten metres aft and is estimating where the ship's nose is. The lockmaster does not guess. He paces precisely beside the ship's forward flagstaff.

Four cables are lowered through fairleads to the linesmen below. The linesmen loop the cables around the bollards. The two aft cables are winched taut.

"Ten metres, ten."

How can that much bulk going at that speed stop in less than 40 feet? It can't be done.

"Five metres, five."

The ship's engines are in full reverse. All four winches on deck are tightening the cables.

"Three metres, three."

"One metre, one."

There is a long silence. A few moments ago the high black hulk seemed to be going too fast. Now it's motionless.

"In position." The yellow ten-metre mark is directly under the ship's prow. Four taut cables strain from the bollards to the deck winches to hold the ship. Was there a slight edge of triumph in the lockmaster's voice? It's hard to tell when it's electronically amplified. Was there a proud glow for a moment from the bridge of the ship?

"Close the upper end."

The heavy sector gates 30 feet under water roll silently out from the sidewalls and meet at the centre of the lock behind the *Algoport*. The upstream safety cable jack-knifes into position. The voice of the lock motorman in the control tower booms out.

"Upper end closed."

"Open the lower end. Cast off number four wire."

As the downstream lock gates open, the linesmen fling the four heavy steel cables off the bollards, the one at the stern first so it won't get caught in a turning propeller if it should plop into the water. The deck winches haul in the cables. The diesel throb accelerates.

"Lower end open."

"Cast off."

The *Algoport* propellers churn the lock into a cauldron of frothy green. It is the end of "B" shift.

Let the weekend begin.

8   *Factory-Outlet Chic*

"I VE GOT SHEETS I haven't used yet. I just keep coming back. You never can tell what they'll have on special."

"Hey, I got boxer shorts, three pair for four dollars. Can't do that in T.O."

"See these? North Stars. Guess what I paid. Go ahead, guess."

"Forty-five?"

"Twenty-two thirty at the factory."

Don't laugh. You'll dance all night in your Bata discontinueds.

And don't pretend you didn't buy them at the factory-outlet store in Batawa. Trim matrons from Ottawa brag openly about their Warner's factory-second "intimate wear." Bargain hunters from Ogdensburg with robust U.S. dollars go home with imperfect Lady Hathaway blouses and brand-name blue jeans without labels. Newlyweds from Montreal sleep in Texmade bedsheets whose flaws are hard to find. Former yuppies from Toronto sew the hems on Caldwell towels.

There are 14 factory-outlet stores between the Quebec border and the Metro Zoo. Like the roadside fruit and vegetable stand, the factory-outlet store has become a destination all its own, an event for the restless urban shopping guerrilla.

You don't have to "know somebody in the business" to get a deal any more. The factory-outlet store offers deals to everybody. The difference between factory-outlet shopping and city shopping is the fact that you know what you are getting in the factory-outlet store. You can usually spot the minute flaws in the bedsheet, the unfinished hems on the bath towels, the trivial defect in the trim on the walking shoe. And you know you can't get your money back.

Factory-outlet shoppers tend to be more observant of details, more aware of what things cost back in the city and are ready to make the trade-off: lower prices in exchange for serviceable merchandise with liveable flaws.

Factory-outlet stores are remote, sometimes hard to find. They offer a challenge to the Toronto subway rider, the Fairview Mall shopper.

There is some ambiguity in the minds of the manufacturers who own these stores. The publisher of *Buyer's Guide to Factory Outlets* says "recent economic conditions have helped factory outlets enjoy increased sales. Since Seconds and overruns are a similar percentage of production from year to year, factory outlets have generally been stocking more merchandise Firsts."

Apparently this stimulates word-of-mouth advertising. Eventually the wholesalers and city retailers, who have been selling the manufacturer's Firsts all these years, complain about the business volume being taken from them by the factory that keeps its factory outlet open Saturdays, Sundays and most long weekends.

One factory outlet visible from the 401 is the Caldwell mill at Iroquois. When times are good the employees' parking lot is packed with cars and pick-ups, the bargain hunters' Volvos and Rabbits.

Caldwell is a part of the Dominion Textile group of companies, so this outlet offers Wabasso, Texmade, Penmans and other brand-name merchandise as well as Caldwell linen and bath towels. Every year the Caldwell outlet has a monster clearance sale in the community building in Iroquois, where they sell unfinished bath towels by the kilo in clear plastic bags. You have to know how to slither the towels around inside the plastic so you can be sure of the colours you are buying.

Joan Ault is the only manager the Caldwell store has had. For 15 years she has been responsible for stocking, displaying and merchandising the increasing variey of goods from Iroquois and

Joan Ault and Kevin Casselman, Caldwell Outlet Store,
Iroquois.

all the other mills and factories in the Dominion Textile group.

Mrs. Ault is the saleswoman you dream of after you have been ignored, snubbed and insulted by the over-dressed, over-made-up lady at Hazelton Lanes.

Mrs. Ault keeps a cordial distance between her and her browsing customers. She knows prices. She knows what's in stock and what's not. She has a "back home" trustworthy style as she discusses sheet patterns or men's and women's sizes in cotton draw-string work pants.

Arthur Ault, Joan's husband, is a mechanic in the weave room at the mill and their son, Kevin, works in the sewing room. Ault is a name that occurs again and again in this part of the country. Ault is the name of one of the founding families along the St. Lawrence river shore. There was a town of Aultsville once, but its site was flooded when Lake St. Lawrence was created from the building of the Seaway. The Aultsville railway station was moved before the flood and is now a part of Upper Canada Village. Ault Foods Limited in Winchester became big and prosperous enough to be bought out by Labatts of London.

Another of the pioneer names in the region is Casselman and Kevin Casselman clerks in the Caldwell factory outlet with Mrs. Ault. Kevin, married three years ago, moved from Morrisburg to Iroquois "to be closer to the job and because real estate was getting expensive in Morrisburg."

Corbron Foundries Ltd. does not have a clearly defined retail area where you can inspect the full line of Chaleureux wood stoves. Instead, you are taken through a metal-lined door into the shipping room to view the different models as they leave the foundry. Corbron is on the Boundary road just outside Cornwall.

The Chaleureux wood stove – in spite of its "picturesque sculptured door design" – is not going to win any awards for beauty; but it apparently wins awards for efficiency. It is the stove bought in truckloads to be sold in Sears' retail outlets across the country.

Stove shoppers usually get one of the owners of the foundry – Nusri or Theodore Abraham – to describe the differences between models. Theodore is the shy one, but once he gets warmed up he is as articulate as his brother, Nusri.

Nusri explains that Abraham is not one of the "first families" of the region, although the Abrahams have been in Cornwall for a long time. His mother and father were immigrants from Lebanon who settled first on a farm near Swift Current in Saskatchewan.

"Abraham is not our family name. When our mother and father came to Canada they could not speak English. Not only that, their last name was difficult for strangers to pronounce. Every time an official asked what his last name was, or his given name, or family name, my father would answer; but the only word the officials heard was his first name, Abraham, so that became our name in Canada."

The Abrahams' life on the prairies was not easy. In those days, there were few doctors. The children were born across the border in Montana. Mrs. Abraham often went to her relatives in Boston to convalesce from childbirth. Finally, she issued an ultimatum to her husband in Swift Current. She could not go back out west. The father sold the farm and travelled east to Cornwall. Life in eastern Ontario was not always easy either, however. Nusri remembers business dealings that foundered because it was assumed the Abrahams were Jews.

Theodore and Nusri Abraham and their fuel-efficient "Chaleureux" wood stove, Boundary Road, Glengarry County.

"Nobody had ever heard of the Maronite Christians of Lebanon."

Theodore designed the Chaleureux stove. The brothers won a patent infringement case in Quebec a few years ago. Nusri developed a chimney cleaner from foundry by-products. The cleaner is marketed in small black plastic containers in the shape of a pot-bellied stove.

Nusri is torn between the attractions of retiring to a small shop where he would make musical instruments, or expanding into the manufacture of houseboats. He used to make violins. He met a Japanese violin maker at a convention in Ottawa one time and shipped some seasoned old lumber to him in Tokyo. The houseboat idea blossomed just as the '82 recession occurred.

The foundry is full of stove bodies waiting to be finished.

He hasn't made up his mind yet.

Mabel Reed has made up her mind. She just loves being in charge of the factory outlet at the Fischl Glove Company in Prescott. Mrs. Reed is one of those confident, well-informed and therefore reassuring retailers who can explain the varieties of leathers, show you the slight colour blemish, demonstrate craftsmanship and deal with the tricky problem of fit.

Mabel Reed, Fischl Glove Factory Store, Prescott.

On the outside, the Fischl Glove Factory is unchanged nineteenth-century factory architecture. It lies beside the railway at the top of George Street. The last hundred yards before you arrive at its door are a torture track of ancient potholes. Inside, the boutique is little more than a short corridor between the plant and the administration office; but it is crowded with gloves, hats and scarves. Once you are in, there is no escape. The closet

Glove factory, Prescott.

intimacy forces you to find your glove size and try them on.

The Fischls arrived in Canada from Czechoslovakia 55 years ago – the same time as the Bata family and for the same reasons. At one time there were a hundred skilled glovemakers at Fischl's. The world has changed. Now much of the fine work is done in Korea, Hong Kong and the Philippines.

Sometimes during their buying trips the Fischls will come across a few pieces of fine lamb or calfskin leather and will design elegant ladies' gloves in such limited quantities they are sold only in the factory outlet.

Mrs. Reed enjoys talking about the craftsmanship and quality of the leather gloves but her face lights up when she talks about her collection of dolls. She has 40 now. Elsi Jones, who teaches dollmaking in Maitland, casts the arms, legs, torsos and heads. Mrs Reed paints the fleshtones and faces and designs and sews their clothing.

When the four women from Ogdensburg were in the shop the other morning, Mrs. Reed sprinkled her conversation freely with "love" and "dear" as she showed fine calfskin gauntlets for women, deerskin for men.

What attracted the women from Ogdensburg?

"It's an outing, love. They're having a marvellous time. They bought some lovely gloves. Now they're off to the hotel in Cardinal for lunch. They serve lovely food there. You should try it, dear."

9   *The River*

T HE TOUR GUIDE, Joe Pereira, did everything he could, but the beautiful woman from West Germany would have to translate her thoughts on North America to herself. She didn't seem to mind.

She was travelling alone so the couples on the package tour had made an effort to draw her into their conversations. She had a German-English dictionary in her hand most of the time. When the hesitant, child-like conversations lapsed into awkward silences, she would smile and excuse herself from the group. On the fan deck of *Thousand Islander IV* she consulted the dictionary dutifully and watched Gananoque diminish as the ship set out on the three-hour cruise. Pereira went back onto the lower deck where the other 36 members of his group were watching the islands and summer homes slide by. They wondered, out loud, if lunch would be ready soon.

The touring group is mostly affluent New Yorkers. Travellers from Australia, South Africa, Bermuda, Switzerland and Germany – on longer North American tours – add this seven-day side trip because it takes them into Canada. It's like getting two foreign countries for the price of one.

Called "Niagara – Ontario," it is organized by New York's Tauck Tours, the only foreign tour Tauck offers. A 44-seat air-conditioned bus leaves New York city six times a week. Corning, New York, is the first sleep stop. On the second day the group visits Niagara Falls, then goes to Toronto for two nights. On day four, the bus rolls into the parking lot at the Gananoque Boat Lines in time for the 11:30 cruise and lunch on board. The group sleeps in Ottawa that night and rolls on to Montreal for two nights. It is a luxury package. It includes the most expensive hotels in the four cities.

"Thirty to forty percent of these people are repeat clients of ours," Pereira says. "Tauck is one of the best in the business. They should be, after 60 years. They've offered this Niagara – Ontario package now for 25 years. They're a terrific outfit to work for. I'll be on this tour all summer." He finishes the homemade cake and sips the coffee politely. He moves easily from table to table fielding questions about Canadian beer, that night's hotel in Ottawa, the international boundary in the Thousand Islands.

Two decks up – behind the wheelhouse – the gang from Vaudreuil High relishes the brisk wind and tanning sun. Some of them pause in their conversations to listen to the public address system. It gives a description in French of the islands, their history and the summer homes along the river.

The maths and science teacher, Robert Sananes, bends low under the yellow nylon rope that is supposed to keep the general public out of the wheelhouse. He steps in and introduces himself to Captain Mangan. Sananes explains that he used to be a ship's officer before he became a schoolteacher.

Courteously, Captain Mangan invites *le professeur* to take the wheel. Moving downstream, *Thousand Islander IV* enters the Seaway channel, marked by red buoys on the left and green

Jamie McLellan, Robert Sananes at the wheel and Marty Mangan.

buoys on the right. Far ahead in the narrow channel an upbound freighter comes into view. The students hang out over the railing of the top deck to watch her approach. The glistening aluminum cruise ship and the rusty old freighter exchange whistle blasts. The Vaudreuil students wave enthusiastically. Their teacher, Mr. Sananes, is at the wheel and he smiles a little worldly smile. He is reminiscent of early Victor Mature.

The gang from Vaudreuil High – before.

The gang from Vaudreuil High – after.

Captain Mangan.

"I was born in Morocco, Tangier. I still ship out as a replacement now and then; but just on the river."

Four of his students and a teaching colleague come up to the wheelhouse and ask permission to come in and photograph *le professeur* while he is at the wheel. He grins proudly now as the little cameras flash. He and Captain Mangan shake hands and smile easily across the language barrier.

Boathouse in a hidden channel, Admiralty Islands,
Gananoque, Leeds County.

Captain Marty Mangan is a teacher in the Leeds Grenville Board
of Education system. He is responsible for "alternative schooling" in Gananoque. He tutors and supervises the work of young
people who, for a variety of reasons, don't fit into traditional
school settings. Part of the curriculum in alternative schooling
puts the pupils into jobs in stores, warehouses and factories in
the district to give them an understanding of "life in the real

world." Mangan's satisfaction comes when one of the employers tells him he wants to hire the student-employee and pay him the going wage for full-time work.

At the same time, Mangan is a river rat. His home is on the river. He has "inland waters papers." He and his wife and another couple holiday in the Rideau system in a 32-footer. Last year was a sabbatical year for him and he crossed the Atlantic in a Belgian freighter.

The three-hour cruise is nearly over. *Thousand Islander IV* threads through a narrow channel and turns towards Gananoque. From this distance it is an idyllic waterfront with great green leafy trees shading the shoreline. One church spire rises above the treetops. Gordon's Marina, the municipal wharf and the old blue tugboat are in the foreground.

"See the green roofs over there? That's where we live." Captain Mangan points to a group of houses with a clear view of the bay and of the town shoreline. "Every time I come in this way, I resent those condos." His finger centres out two bare squat buildings under construction beside the Thousand Islands Playhouse. "They don't fit in, somehow. It just doesn't look the same."

Two decks below, Joe Pereira tips the woman in charge of the snack bar and goes out on the fan deck to shepherd his well-heeled flock. The beautiful woman from West Germany has put the German-English dictionary away in her purse. The language of bright sun, beautiful islands, scintillating water does not need subtitles. The "activity day" for the Vaudreuil students will be over soon. The tourists and the students leave *Islander IV* and stroll slowly across the grass to their busses.

When all the passengers have gone ashore, Captain Wilfred Bilow comes aboard. He is the chief engineer of Gananoque Boat Lines and *Islander IV* is one of the four cruise ships he keeps in shape for the May to October tourist season.

"We work on these boats constantly. We are always doing something to make them easier to operate, to make them more comfortable for the passengers." He climbs backwards down the narrow passageway to the engine room.

"These two diesels have been in operation for 11 years now and we haven't done anything to them. We inspect them on a regular basis, but we haven't had to do anything major to them in all those years. I remember I put an air intake on this one a few years ago, but I took it off last year. It was an unnecessary complication. Now the main air intake provides the air for all three engines."

"This one," Captain Bilow stares glumly at the third big Caterpillar marine diesel, "is a different story. Every year since it came out of the factory we've had to replace a part. That's new last year. Twenty-three hundred bucks." He points to a small attachment on the side of the cylinder block. "There, two years ago, eleven hundred."

"This engine is the identical twin of that one; but it's been a temperamental cuss." Still, he is loyal to Caterpillar. "Think of it this way, one of these engines does the same work as a truck

Homeward bound.

Captain Bilow

diesel hauling a load up a steep grade for 175,000 miles."

Not counting the hand-held fire extinguishers on the boat, there are four separate fire prevention and extinguishing systems in the engine room. Captain Bilow checks them all.

Back up on deck, he wishes there were a carpeting that would last longer under the punishment of the sun, the rain and the thousands of tourists every day from May to October.

He sidles in behind the snack bar. Until this year it was a problem. When the hull was first being fitted out, Captain Bilow had offered two designs for the snack bar. The boss had selected the design which jutted into the centre passageway, making it awkward for tourists to line up for food and drinks. The design was wrong and the snack bar remained clumsy until he decided last winter to make the bar longer and narrower, with an unobstructed passageway for the customers and just enough space behind for waiters to serve 500 passengers.

"See? It's much simpler. Makes it better for the waiters, better for the paying customers."

Up in the wheelhouse there are two high swivel chairs with padded backs and arm rests, a radar scope, two radio sets, and an upholstered sofa for a captain who might grab a few minutes rest between cruises. The control panel has three sets of dials, one for each engine. The throttles are within reach of the big chromed wheel.

The wheelhouse has a stripped-down look to it. The only things that seem out of place are some plastic coffee cups on a small shelf, some hand-made posters making fun of crew members, and a small round box of chewing tobacco sitting atop a well-thumbed copy of *Know Your Ships: A Listing of Vessels Passing through the United States and Canadian Locks.*

Although he tries to hide it, Captain Bilow has an almost emotional attachment to the four *Thousand Islanders* in the cruise fleet. He was one of the central figures in their construction so he knows every weld, every pipe, every built-in detail. He is an encyclopaedia of diesel power, radar, navigation, catering, housekeeping, fire prevention, welding, naval architecture, electronics and electricity. His associates say he has a natural affinity for things mechanical.

"I'm like my father was. Not much formal education; but there's very little I can't learn." Before the next load of tourists comes on board, he goes ashore, jumps in the pick-up and drives back to the Boat Lines shop where *Islanders I, II and III* are waiting for his attention. "Oh yes, I have my papers and I used to take my turn on the cruises when we just had two boats. Now, with four, I'm full time keeping things in shape here. Let the young fellows skipper the boats."

The minute hand on the clock in the wheelhouse is approaching the half hour. Everybody is on board, except four tourists running from the ticket office to the dock. The engines hum quietly. The forward lines have been cast off. The wind is quickly blowing the bow away from the tie wall. The loudspeaker link between the bridge and the fan deck is open.

"Do you want to wait for them?"

"Yes."

"Then keep your stern in."

"Keep her back. We'll see if they can get on."

"Keep her coming. You're four feet off."

"Let all the lines go."

"Back slow." The late tourists step aboard.

"All clear! That wind'll take you off the dock. She's all yours."

It is Jamie's voice from the stern of *Islander IV*. It is Marty Mangan's voice from the bridge. He is making his second trip of the day.

Jamie jumps lightly across the space between the dock and the stern, secures the gate and climbs up to the wheelhouse to stand beside Captain Mangan as he takes the ship away from Gananoque and downstream towards Boldt Castle.

There are small crescents of tobacco stain at the corners of Jamie's mouth. Captain Mangan reaches over and picks up the box of chewing tobacco. He looks at it and shakes his head.

"How can you chew this stuff. It's disgusting."

No answer; just a sheepish smile.

"Show me your teeth. Let me have a look at your gums."

Another smile.

"Your teeth are going to fall out. Your gums are going to rot. There was a story on *60 Minutes* last Sunday. They showed the sores kids get on the inside of their mouths from chewing that stuff. Imitating the old baseball players and rodeo cowboys who advertise the stuff. Come on, Jamie, you don't need that crap."

"Yeah, my mouth gets a little sore." Jamie runs a hand through his straw-coloured hair. In his white shirt, blue tie, gold epaulettes, he looks like the young first officer on an E-boat being upbraided by his admiral in an old World War II movie. He will quit chewing tobacco when he sees the *60 Minutes* rerun this summer.

Captain Mangan reaches up and changes radio frequency channels on the ship's radio so he can listen to ships in the Seaway talking to the control tower at St. Lambert. One of his friends is an American pilot who takes ships from Cape Vincent to Montreal. Mangan recognizes the voice.

After a long winter the boat tour season on the river is getting under way at last. Captain Mangan is in command today, but there are three other GBL captains on board. It's good to see the season start again after the long winter lay-up.

The boat passes buoy number 18. Captain Mangan starts the tape machine that puts a bilingual description of the tour into the ship's public address system.

Buoy number 18, and three thousand more just like it along the Seaway, were put in position by the Canadian Coast Guard work boat from the Prescott base as soon as the ice was out of the river.

Three thousand! Some with steady lights the big ships steer by; some with flashing lights to caution the ship's pilot. The floating buoys come mostly in red (keep them on your right when you are going upstream), or green (keep them on your left when you are going upstream). There are others painted red and green, yellow, yellow and black, orange and white and plain white. They come in different shapes too. There are pillars, cans, spars, cones and spheres. Most of them are anchored along the edges of the Seaway channels. Some of the lights are shore-based in red and white towers made from steel road culverts.

It wouldn't be a Seaway without them.

This is Hubert Casselman's world. Hubert and his crews are busiest from Christmas to April Fool's Day. Seaway traffic stops at Christmas time and starts up again in the last two weeks of March. Then blacksmiths, welders, machinists, carpenters, tinsmiths, radar technicians, engine mechanics, captains and deckhands hustle to get the buoys out of the river, back to the Coast Guard base at Prescott, for rehabilitation and replacement. They need fresh paint, new long-life batteries, anchor chains, anchors.

Hubert is the yard maintenance foreman at the base. His handiwork marks the fairways in Lake St. Louis, Lake St. Francis, Lake St. Lawrence, the approaches to the locks, the narrow channel winding through the Thousand Islands, the approaches to the Welland lock system and along Lake Erie's shore.

It wouldn't be a Seaway without him. Watching Hubert Casselman in action is like watching all the macho, gonzo he-men in all the beer commercials on television. He has the gusto, husky élan, all-out joie de vivre that brewmasters love. The image is misleading. Hubert doesn't drink.

He was born on a farm near Inkerman. He fits the tradition of farm boys who left the family farm to make successful careers on the sea.

He started out as a section hand with the CPR, then joined the Coast Guard when the St. Lawrence Seaway Authority started to build the Montreal – Lake Ontario leg.

In supertanker figures, ships have made about 150,000 transits of the Seaway since the Queen and President Eisenhower opened it in 1959. In those 26 seasons well over a billion metric tonnes

Hubert Casselman.

of cargo have been shipped through the Seaway. The ups and downs of Seaway shipments are an accurate gauge of world trade. If the Russians buy less wheat from the Americans, Seaway tonnage goes down dramatically. If U.S. manufacturers use the strong U.S. dollar to buy cheaper foreign steel, then Seaway tonnage rises. Upbound iron ore shipments usually increase just before any boom in U.S. car sales.

The Seaway's bread and butter revenue comes from bulk cargoes like wheat and other grains, iron ore, coal, salt, fuel oil.

Big is beautiful on the Seaway. In a typical season it sees 3,5000 loaded ships carrying 55,000,000 metric tonnes. The ship-

pers pay, on average, about $1.50 a tonne. Ships are getting bigger so the total tonnage of cargo increases, even though the number of ships declines a little each year.

The depth of the Seaway from Montreal to Duluth is crucial to its utility. In 1967 the maximum permissible ship draft was increased from 25 feet 6 inches to 25 feet 9 inches. Those three extra inches meant the big ships could each carry an additional 300 tonnes of cargo.

When Hubert Casselman joined the Coast Guard in Preston,

the biggest ship on the old canal system was 140 feet long and carried 750 tonnes of cargo.

Today his spars, buoys and fixed navigation aids mark a channel that will handle hulls 730 feet long, each carrying 28,000 tonnes of cargo. Multiply the length by five and you can multiply the payload by thirty-five.

Hubert Casselman is another one of those fathers who made his work interesting for his children. One son, Paul, works at the base in Prescott. Another son, Kevin, is a crew-member on the *Simcoe*, a small Coast Guard ice-breaker.

It wouldn't be a Seaway without them.

10   *Not a Bad Guy*

HE WAS THIN, blonde, sun-baked and 20. His skintight jeans had the right amount of fade. He held his thumb out low, down by his knee. Cool. When he jack-knifed into the car his knees jammed against the glove compartment. He must be the high-school basketball star.

He sure as hell was not planning to be a farmer. He was born and grew up on a farm north of Brockville, still lives there, as a matter of fact, but he's getting out. He wants to live in town. He was hitch-hiking down to Brockville for the night shift at the Duncan Hines cookie factory. If he got there early he'd visit his girlfriend for a while.

He got the job on the cookie packaging line at Duncan Hines a year ago. They told him then the job would be good for at least three years. Then the other day he reads in the paper the line was going to be automated. He doesn't know whether he still has a job or not.

He hopes Black and Decker will be taking on people. His father used to work there and his sister works there now. Black and Decker bought the small appliances division of General Electric and there was talk they were going to close down the G-E plant in Barrie and move all the manufacturing to Brockville.

He likes the job at Duncan Hines. Nine at night until nine in the morning for two nights, then two days off.

The hitch-hiker had gone to Pineview Elementary School in Athens. That's as far as he got in school. He remembers one teacher from his last year, Truesdell. Coached the basketball teams. Not a bad guy.

David Truesdell lives most of every day in a red and white track suit because – as well as teaching his home-room class – he teaches phys. ed. at Pineview and does a lot of coaching after school. When he first went to Pineview he inherited discipline problems. His predecessor, "well, he sort of let things go. The kids wouldn't take off their toques or galoshes in class and they tried to pull the same stuff on me." It took him a couple of months to show the kids he was not last year's pushover. They took their toques and galoshes off and got into the habit of calling him sir.

David Truesdell commutes the 35 miles between Gananoque

David Truesdell, Pineview Elementary School, Athens.

and Athens, usually by the Mallorytown Road, but when the snow is bad he takes 401, 29 and 42. The only thing that can keep him from making it is a freezing-rain storm. The yellow busses don't roll then either.

"I like the commute. You get to see the seasons changing. I saw three deer yesterday morning and again last night on the way home."

There were eight kids in the Truesdell family in Ivy Lea. Their father was a transport driver who worked for Direct Winters and Smith Transport, in the days when it was all gearing down and gearing up through the little towns along old number two between Montreal and Toronto.

"We were river rats. Swimming was second nature for us. The river was our natural playground, and it's where I'll go when I finish teaching. My brother and I run a yacht rental business."

The Truesdells are grown now. One works for a municipal government. Two are in real estate. One studies economics at Carleton. Another has a welding business and one is learning to be a fish and wildlife specialist. David got his B.A. in geography at Carleton University, then went for his B.Ed. and a specialist rating in phys. ed. at McArthur Hall in Kingston.

His teaching style is physical. He spends little time at the desk. He cruises the chalk boards, writing key words, underlin-

David Truesdell cruising the chalk boards.

ing, asking the kids questions while he looks at the outline on the board. He assumes everyone in the class has read what they were supposed to read, so his tone of voice implies he expects the answer fast. The questions tumble out, one on top of the other. The grade six and seven pupils are caught up in his pace. It is a contest.

The classroom windows are open and the playground fills up

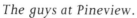
The guys at Pineview.

with the students from the other classes in the 12-room school. Teachers stop to lean into Truesdell's class.

"Come on, David, come on, we're waiting."

He keeps them waiting. There are more social studies ques-

Phys. Ed.

tions that have to be answered before his class can leave to watch the senior races that he will supervise.

The whole school turns out for the races. Nobody is in a hurry to get home. The young jocks cluster around Truesdell as he

After school, Pineview.

checks off the runners. He looks at his watch and calls to the starter: "Line 'em up, line 'em up. Let's go. I've got Blue Jay tickets for tonight. I've got to be on the 401 by five o'clock."

Not a bad guy.

11   *Notes from a Glass Dance Floor*

THE MAVERICKS ARE READY for their first set of the night at the Flying Dutchman Motel. It is too early in the season for the summer people from Butternut Bay, but a good crowd of locals has turned out. The reflecting ball is turning. The lights under the glass dance floor flash murkily on and off: navigation aids for the awkward and the uncertain.

Gail Lynch, the drummer and singer, settles into the *boom-chick, boom-chick* country rhythm. Murray McDonald matches it on rhythm guitar. Tom Smith plays lead guitar. John Purdon sings and plays bass guitar. Steve Ball crouches happily over the keyboards.

John introduces "some belly rubbing music that goes something like this." Four couples jitterbug in slow motion to the *boom-chick, boom-chick* beat. Steve turns around to count the dancers. It's how you judge. Not an easy way to make a living.

Purdon is the leader of The Mavericks. He books them into lounges, dances and weddings anywhere between Kemptville and Oshawa. When a tavern owner books a group he gets a

Steve Ball, maverick on the keyboards.

special permit from the Liquor Licensing Board and he pays a fee to the musicians' and composers' union. If the group does not attract a crowd, well, it's a long time between bookings.

In blue shirts and blue unbuttoned vests that are green in the dim fluorescent light, The Mavericks don't look like urban cowboys, nor like a mismatched shirt-and-blue-jeans group. They are somewhere in the middle with their music too.

Steve Ball is 20 and wants to write contemporary rock songs. He plays country and middle-of-the-road rock in lounges in Cornwall, Prescott, Gananoque, Kingston, Belleville, Oshawa and here at Butternut Bay. He has played with the Charisma group in Belleville and with Tracks, with Terry Carisse, in Ottawa.

A Yamaha electronic grand takes up most of the entrance hall in his apartment in Kingston. He keeps two notebooks for phrases and ideas and lyrics. He props the words up on the Yamaha and chords his way slowly through each line, hunting for a melody line that will match the phrasing of the words. Sometimes he gets together with other musicians to work on music for his lyrics.

Music is like breathing in the Ball home in Joyceville. Steve's mother, Beth, sings in the Seeley's Bay United Church Choir. She studied music theory and the history of jazz at Queen's University. Both his mother and father encouraged him through nine years of piano lessons. His brothers, David and Derek, are taking piano lessons now.

"They kind of look up to me, I guess."

The dance is a grave mixture of '40s jitterbugging and the two-step from Gilley's Bar. The music is Willy Nelson, Merle Haggard, Gordon Lightfoot, Eddy Rabbit, Johnny Cash, Roger Miller, Kenny Rogers – and Lance Russwurm.

Fridays and Saturdays, Lance Russwurm is one of the four musicians who, as The Neon Nites, take their electric guitars and drums to play in almost forgotten towns and villages.

Over in Mennonite country, it's The Country Connection, The Good Brothers and The Neon Nites who play loud enough to make you shout when you're talking and slow enough to let you and your dance partner do your own weird thing. No glass tiles flash in the tiny dance floor; but you can play billiards or skittles at the St. Clement's Tavern. Friday and Saturday nights they offer all-you-can-eat schnitzel for $3.95. It's $4.50 for half a dozen sweet and tender ribs.

The long tables are crowded. The music is well amplified. Lance's diction is good, the words to the songs are clear; but

tonight the customers would rather shout than dance.

Between bookings of The Neon Nites, Lance works patiently at his graphic art. He uses a hot electric needle to draw Mennonite country images on wood. His drawing board is in the Hunzberger Gallery in St. Jacob's. Every summer tourists file through the gallery, stand at his elbow and lean over his shoulder to watch the drawing take shape on the wood.

Lynn Russwurm.   *Lance Russwurm.*

A similar cultural intimacy can be found at the Thousand Islands Playhouse on the Gananoque waterfront.

The first act of Noel Coward's *Hay Fever* ends when the maid struggles across the stage with the baggage of all the loathsome visitors who arrive at the English country house for the weekend. The houselights come up at the end of the act yet she is still wrestling with the big 1930s valises. At this playhouse, the people in the first row of the theatre audience jump up on stage to help the maid with her task.

Lance Russwurm of the "Neon Nites."

"That's dramatic involvement of the highest order," Marjorie Preston says proudly. She plays the part of the grouchy little maid.

In the other life that practically all actors have, Marjorie Preston is married to Richard Preston, a distinguished historian who is writing the history of the Royal Military College at Kingston.

Marjorie is part of a success story in Canadian theatre. The Thousand Islands Playhouse does not lose money. With a season

Dick and Marjorie Preston.

as long as Stratford's, it lures regular subscribers from further and further away every year.

The Playhouse is small, in the tradition of summer stock. The 280 seats have an unobstructed view of the actors. It is a thrust stage, close to the audience – there is no room for any other kind. Backstage is for thin actors, thin costume fitters, thin make-up artists. It is the second floor of the Gananoque Canoe Club, on the waterfront between Gordon's Marina and the Ontario Provincial Police boat house.

"The only real difference between the Kennedy Centre on the Potomac and the Playhouse on the St. Lawrence is that the St. Lawrence is bigger," says Greg Wanless, the Playhouse's artistic director.

The dream of the founding fathers of the Playhouse was to break even, at least, by persuading the American and Canadian owners of the summer homes on the Thousand Islands to bring their weekend guests to the theatre by boat, tie up at the Play-

Queen's University drama student helps artistic director Greg Wanless build set for Thousand Islands Playhouse.

house dock, promenade on the porches and dock at intermission, enjoy the play and go home. The break-even part of the dream came true but not the way the dreamers thought it would.

The local people are the supporters of theatre in Gananoque. The summer people haven't gotten into the habit yet.

12　The Great-Horned Dilemma

I T BEGAN NINE YEARS AGO when a bedraggled little robin was brought to the Chubb doorstep. That was when they decided to start caring for orphaned or injured birds.

Six more birds were brought to them that year for rehabilitation and foster care. The same year, they slowly unravelled government licensing complexities and explored the mysteries of fund-raising. They finally got the licence that permits them to care for wild birds indoors.

At first glance the aviary looks like Dogpatch. A tangle of woven-wire and two-by-four add-ons adorns the back of the Chubbs' split-level bungalow. But there is sense to the arrangement of cages that have sprouted. Different bird species need different spaces for exercising their wings and for keeping their legs and feet healthy. Many of the birds here are fed through artfully contrived apertures. Some cages have double sets of screen doors to prevent the birds from escaping when Kit or Robin Chubb go into them. Other cages have one-way glass so the birds will never see humans at all.

The Chubbs decided to start their compassion-driven aviary because there wasn't anyone else around willing to do it. As soon as people heard about it, the number of orphans and cripples climbed: from six the first year to 60 in the second, 140 in the third and 400 birds in the fourth year.

By writing notes in minute detail on each "patient" and storing the notes in a computer, "Kit" Chubb has accumulated a unique data base. Problems are identified much more quickly now. Solutions come to hand more deftly.

It is a "good news, bad news" world at the Chubbs'. For example, the good news is that they were able to rehabilitate a rare white pelican that had crash-landed on highway 401 near Kingston. It had been blown off its course in Minnesota by strong west winds.

Nobody knows exactly what broke the pelican's wing. It could have been a power line or a car or the impact of a dry landing on the highway. The 401 may have looked like a waterway in the bad weather.

The white pelican is an endangered species. This one was back in flying shape after two weeks of tender loving care at the Chubbs' aviary. The World Wildlife Fund and the Canada Life Assurance Company paid for the bird's jet flight to a Florida bird rehabilitation centre and its eventual release.

The bad news is the fact that the pelican – like all birds – has a short gut so it dropped great white excretions of fish dinner every ten minutes of its stay in the aviary. Clean-up never seemed to stop.

The Chubbs have treated 143 different species of wild birds so far at their Avian Care and Research Foundation. The causes of injury are a colossal lament of natural misfortune and human thoughtlessness, neglect and irrational fear. Leghold-trapped in Quebec. Hit by a car. Shot. Dying of starvation. Liver disease. Blasted through the chest with a rifle. Shotgun pellets. Caught in a spider's web. Shot in the wing. Beak and neck tangled in a nylon fishing line. Hooked on barbed wire.

The wild birds come from Montreal, Sudbury, Toronto, Lind-

Kit Chubb and the Orphan from Wales Island.

say and all the counties along the 401 from the Quebec border to Toronto. A Georgia trucker brought a bird from his southern home to be mended by the Chubbs.

A group of 150 volunteer drivers in Ontario and Quebec have organized themselves into the "Flying Angels." When someone reports an injured or orphaned bird to the Chubbs, the map pinned on the wall beside the phone shows the nearest "flying angel." The angel picks up the bird and brings it to the aviary – the last house on the right as you leave Verona, going north on highway 38.

Downstairs, "Kit" has her office. Near it are the nurseries for the lab mice – daily diet for the ailing hawks and owls. There are some small bird cages, where a downed flicker has developed an annoying habit of banging the metal with his beak. In the corner of a tiny, meticulous room, space has been made for Mrs. Chubb's drawing board. She is a talented artist. Reproductions of her drawings and watercolours are sold to raise money for the aviary.

Upstairs Robin Chubb, architect, runs a compact office. Today he is going to Sydenham for the opening of tenders from contractors bidding on a community centre he has designed. Last week he and "Kit" drove up to Maberly to talk to members of the Rideau Valley Naturalists Club. When the Chubbs give a lecture they usually take along a rough-legged hawk that came to them with a dislocated wing. The hawk has turned out to be a docile and approachable "visual aid."

"Kit" Chubb looks you straight in the eye and tells you she is an eccentric. She takes you for a guided tour of the cages, if you appear serious. After she explains what she does for each bird in each cage, she turns out to be certifiably normal. She is doing something nobody else wants to do. She does it well. It has become an integral part of the Chubbs' family life. It keeps her in touch with a wider world.

"It is a lot more fun than housework," she says.

The Foundation has a proper board of directors, including Farley Mowat, but "Kit" and Robin are the active directors. "Ninety percent her; ten percent me," Robin says.

One day last April, "Kit" got the phone call from the Upper Canada Migratory Bird Sanctuary where Bryce Rupert works. They had a baby great-horned owl that, they said, fell from a nest and was found in the undergrowth in a grove of pine trees on Wales Island.

The voice on the phone said the owl was in a small aluminum carrying cage and they were planning to feed it ground beef and water. The phone conversation became a short course in biology.

No, the mother great-horned owl is not likely to feed the baby owl if the baby owl is put back under the pine trees. Owls are not biologically programmed to nurture offspring that have fallen out of the nest, especially if there is another chick still in the nest. It would be better if they got a long ladder and put the baby back in the nest.

No, ground beef cannot be a long-term diet for the bird. Beef

Robin Chubb.

Great-Horned Orphan.

is deficient in the amount of calcium the baby bird needs to develop sturdy bones during the first critical growing weeks. Young owls in their natural habitat get the calcium they need from mice and meadow voles.

Next day a flying angel drives the squawking ball of fluff the 80 miles from Morrisburg to Verona. A mature great-horned owl with an injured wing becomes its foster mother.

One month later the Wales Island baby owl has almost tripled in size. Two bumps of down have started to form on its head. And two more orphaned great-horned babies have been brought to Verona. The foster-mother owl sits high in one corner of the spacious cage. The three babies are on the nest – a platform high in another protected corner.

Just before feeding time, the young owl grips a slanting perch with its talons, stares fiercely out at the intruders on the other side of the cage and scolds with an irregular clicking noise. *Click-tick-tick. Click. Click. Tick.*

The fate of the Wales Island orphan is not clear. Hans Van der Sweet – one of the flying angels in Cornwall – spent an afternoon at Wales Island looking for any trace of an owl nest, of a mother owl who would welcome back her long-lost baby. There was no sign of life on the island.

Can wild foster parents be found somewhere else, to teach it the subtleties of survival?

Maybe.

13   *Exit Ramp 593*

NOWADAYS THE HIGH PRIESTS OF NOSTALGIA are publishers. They do *Organic Gardening and Farming* in Pennsylvania; *Blair and Ketchum's Country Journal* in New England; and *Harrowsmith* magazine in 401 country.

They don't use the word "nostalgia" for fear of being called "quaint"; but they wallow in it month after month.

Nobody makes fun of the past. No matter how recent, no matter how remote, the past is a matter of reverence because it holds roots of our survival. The reasons why we are the way we are lie hidden away in the archives and attics of our ancestors. Whenever a piece of the past survives we treasure it and surround it with myths and legends of craftsmanship, utility, and naive beauty. When it doesn't survive, we reconstruct it. Our cultural saints are archaeologists.

Nobody makes fun of the future, either. The future is a snake pit of dead fish in polluted water, barren side hills that used to be forests, deserts that used to be grain fields, leaky nuclear power plants, incurable social diseases, colliding trains, unfriendly skies, food additives, chemical contaminants in the air we breathe, the water we drink, the earth we cultivate. When part of the future arrives early, some embrace it as a saviour arriving in the nick of time, others deplore it, picket it and sign petitions against it. Futurologists and prognosticators are harbingers of humanity's last stress. Or last hope.

The present contains both. Half in love with the past, half in fear of the future, we tell each other "things ain't what they used to be" and yearn for "the good old days." Life isn't working out as well as it should. We are uncertain. We cling to the past. We exaggerate it and dive with innocent pleasure into the uncontaminated swimming hole of nostalgia. It is our safe haven.

Camden East is a crossroads village in Lennox and Addington County, north of Exit Ramp 593. There is a vintage limestone business block on one corner of the only intersection. Up the hill and to the left, across the Napanee river, there is a vintage red-brick Victorian mansion with a gloomy and romantic history. *Harrowsmith* magazine is published in these two buildings.

Harrowsmith is a successful magazine because its first issues developed a free-form editorial recipe that attracts people who believe "old is best"; new is a gimmick that breaks down just after the warranty runs out. In one article even second-hand tractors were made to seem desirable.

Founding *Harrowsmith* was James Lawrence's exit ramp from the dailiness of life in the editorial offices of the Kingston *Whig Standard*. In each of the early issues, he reported on the problems of starting up the magazine. The magazine's growing pains were carefully a-clutter with the quaint and familiar images of yesterday. He wrote of "a cat who likes to sprawl on just-finished layout boards," "doing business on a rural party telephone," "producing a national magazine in a farmhouse kitchen." "One of Camden East's more sprightly 75-year-olds says he never thought he'd see the day ... " "Our own offices are heated by wood." "We cross the road to use the Texaco station washroom." "An editor can often be found splitting firewood in the sideyard to keep the office airtight stoves fuelled." "The publisher is said to have carried the circulation files around in his hip pocket." "The post mistress might sell you a pound of cheddar cheese." "Ladies' unmentionables are stacked on a shelf behind the old oak mail wicket." At one time the publisher had "an intense desire to

Bookstore, Camden East.

hang a Gone Fishin' sign on the door." Another time he thanked
a neighbour for "allowing us the use of his limestone granary
for back-issue storage."

It is that artful dropping of the letter "g" from the Gone Fishin'
sign that links *Harrowsmith* to the Katzenjammer Kids, the
Toonerville Trolley, Major Hoople, Out Our Way, James Whit-
comb Riley. "Ladies' unmentionables" is a phrase redolent of

the days when pre-teen boys studied the corset pages of Eaton's Catalogue in the backhouse at the corner of the barn.

From the beginning the people at *Harrowsmith* had a clear-eyed vision of what the readers wanted: "the majority of our readers are looking for alternatives"; "the possibility of locating a traditionally urban business or profession in a small town"; "a saner pace of life"; "alternatives to agribusiness and urban living." "We happen to believe life outside the major urban centres is becoming increasingly attractive." "Between the metro highrise apartment and the one-room cabin in the wilds there is a great deal of middle ground."

Growth in circulation brought success to *Harrowsmith*. Success brought along her baggage as well. At the start of the '70s, the editors looked into the future and saw: homeowners turning to alternative forms of energy that cannot be metered; storage systems for solar heat and wood heat becoming more efficient; political and legal wars over the right of small-scale producers of electricity (solar, wind or hydro) to plug into the Ontario Hydro power grid and be paid for their input; chronic gasoline shortages; alcohol-generated fuels from biomass crops on idle farmland; nuclear power in a protracted suicide; a thriving back-to-the-land movement; the solar food-producing greenhouse; and society moving closer to the conserver ethic.

The number of subscribers climbed, the number of pages each month increased and were filled with the real stuff of the conserver ethic: food, food and more food. How to grow it organically, raise and market it successfully. Bees, cheese, watercress, asparagus, wild rice, green tomatoes, boysenberry jam, home-made bread, home-made beer, bean sprouts, maple syrup, canning, gardening, wood-stove cooking, cider, plum pudding, coffee substitutes, hydroponics, organic insect control and self-sufficiency.

Barn and solar architecture, homesteading life style, wood stoves, wood lots, trees, worms, seeds, rural careers, log cabins and lightning are grist for *Harrowsmith*'s editorial mills.

More readers brought with them more advertisers. The advertisers wanted to know what the editorial philosophy of *Harrowsmith* is and who the readers are. *Harrowsmith* wanted to know what the advertisers' corporate views are in case they collide with the views of sensitive seekers-of-alternatives.

In a message to advertisers, *Harrowsmith* said, "Quaint, we are not. Quaint, we never were. Along with its readers, who range from corporate executives to homesteaders, *Harrowsmith* has recognized that society has some backtracking to do, to that sensible middle ground where the air and water are clean and success is measured in terms of quality, not quantity. It may be the stuff that dreams are made from, but is also the stuff from which reality begins.''

Who are *Harrowsmith*'s readers? A few live in the country on small holdings and the magazine is their survival Bible; but most of them live in towns and cities with populations up to 30,000 and in cities with populations between 100,000 and a million. Most of the readers make more than $25,000 a year. Most finished high school and a high percentage went on to get university degrees. They are mostly married and own their homes. They generally have big families which listen to more radio than most and watch less television than you'd expect.

Success at divining the mood of the great middle ground is compounding. *Harrowsmith* is now publishing books for the conserver ethic, has introduced a new magazine, *Equinox*, and has expanded into the United States with an office in Vermont.

Families seat-belted into their Toyotas – "we live for the weekends" – want to get off the four-lane treadmill and find the time warp that will take them back to their roots and reaffirm their belief that "old is best." *Harrowsmith* is their exit ramp for now.

14   *Island of Independents*

CITIES HAVE RAVELLED EDGES where suburbs and country collide in a confusion of farms and welding shops, kennels and golf courses, dead car cemeteries, nurseries and gravel pits, mansions and chicken coops, motels and trailer courts. People rush through them in Friday night summer flight from the melting asphalt. They tear back through them in Sunday night's return to livings that have to be made. Poets don't write sonnets about where cities begin. Songwriters are not inspired by where the country ends.

Islands have neat edges of water – unequivocal water that gives the islander a sharp sense of apartness, of security, of detachment from the mainland's neurosis; of being quietly special because we are here on this island of calm and they are "over there," getting it all wrong. Islands are great places for people with paranoia. Whoever is out to get them will first have to pay a dollar and a quarter to the ferry boat skipper.

All islanders have just one cross to bear and that's the ferry service. The ferry to Amherst Island is never big enough. The service is never often enough. The fare is too high. Islanders suffer these indignities in exchange for the physical and psychological space between their land and the troublesome mainland.

Islanders are jealous lovers. They want the whole world to know all about their serenity; but they don't want the world to come calling too often. There's a limit to the number of slices in the tranquility pie.

Islanders tell each other how fortunate they are. Then they tell each other why they need a bigger, more frequent ferry service to the mainland.

Rev. McIntyre walks four brisk laps around the manse and the Presbyterian cemetery every day. It is part of his valiant struggle to find the lost waistline of his youth. Each time he passes the limestone church, the sun has moved a little towards the west and put a touch more light on the caps of the buttresses. In another twenty minutes the west wall with the rosette window will shimmer in the May sunlight. Your teeth will ache with the whiteness of the limestone.

Twenty or twenty-five people come to St. Paul's Presbyterian

Presbyterian Church, Amherst Island.

Church during the winter. In summer, vacationers and visitors push the congregation up to 60 or 65. Loyal old church members go to unusual lengths to raise money to keep the church in good repair. *The Island Treasure Cook Book* has had four printings and paid for a new organ and broadloom. Voluntarism has been a lifetime characteristic of the church. It was built with limestone quarried and dressed by prisoners at the Kingston penitentiary. The building blocks were skidded across the midwinter ice.

"Living on the island? The only problem is the ferry. If you are going into Kingston for the evening, say a movie, or the theatre, you should be a half hour early at the dock so you don't get left. Trouble is, everybody knows this and gets there half an hour early. It's no good if you have to wait an hour for the next run." The glint in his eye, the good-natured smile show that the complaint is not really a complaint at all. It is the knee-jerk ferryism of the Amherst Islander.

The ferry is the social glue for the islanders. During the 16-minute ride to the mainland, the islander is confined to an even smaller island where the deep and shallow profundities of the day are probed.

The licence plate holder on the car says, "I don't get mad, I get even."

The bumper sticker says, "If it ain't country, it ain't music."

The driver of the pick-up says, "I'm afraid of that nuclear. I'm afraid of anything I can't see. I can see a mad dog. I can see a crazy man coming at me with a knife. I don't like that nuclear."

On the ride back to highway 33, the ferry skipper says, "Don't waste your film on the likes of me." He was on submarine chasers during World War II. "And I spent three months in British E-boats. They sure pounded the daylights out of you." Memories of the war at sea come easily to his mind. It is the anniversary of VE-day.

It is also the day when issue number 88 of *Island Beacon* hits the news stand in Glenn's Store – the only news stand, the only store in Stella, the island's only village. Inside the mimeographed monthly is a paragraph contributed by Kevin McCormick, grade one, Amherst Island Public School.

"On Monday a new person came to school. His name is Ben. He is in grade 3. I think that he is the 2nd or 3rd oldest in grade 3. He is my fifth best friend. I really like his bike, it has handle brakes! Ben is 8 years old. He has brown curly hair and he also has brown eyes."

Amherst Island is like that: innocent, practical, scaled down.

There is nothing for the tourist. There is everything for the tourist. There is uncommercialized space. There are vistas of the lake, Prince Edward County, the mainland, the skyline of Kingston, and sometimes in the foreground the self-important ferry with a good-natured Walter Mitty of a captain at the helm, one eye cocked for the elusive U-boat conning tower.

Susan and Bruce Caughey are the tourist industry on Amherst Island. They offer farm vacations in their 160-year-old limestone house. Their largest single asset is the absence of facilities on the island: no gas station, no film for the camera, no picnic tables. Tourists in search of the country have no alternative but to become a part of it.

Susan Caughey brings a pleasant Indiana gregariousness to the Poplar Dell farm vacation home. The old slipper comfort of family mementoes in the living room is presided over by the Bell upright piano made in Guelph a hundred years ago, and the long church pew beside it.

The island is a haven for hawks and owls. When the meadow vole population is high, hawks in search of dinner glide into the prevailing wind and hang five feet above the community pasture in the centre of the island.

Amherst calls itself the westernmost of the Thousand Islands; but its inhabitants are not frantically concerned with tourist promotion, like people in the Brockville – Gananoque – Kingston area.

Finding Amherst Island's past doesn't take long. The barn architecture is unusual. Each barn has a stone stable at ground level. Some barns have flat stone foundations. There remain a few flat stone fences and one flat stone house. Daniel Fowler, one of the pioneer members of the Royal Canadian Academy, built his home here in 1850. His oil paintings and watercolours of dead game, hollyhocks and the Amherst Island landscape are a part of the country's national heritage.

The least publicized event on Amherst Island is lilac time. Nowhere else in Ontario is there such massive planting of the old familiar bush. Maybe the islanders have stumbled on a tourist promotion formula after all. Relax. Don't do anything special for visitors. Don't tell anyone about the lilacs. Complain a lot about the ferry service.

15   *Apple Blossom Time*

T HERE WAS A TIME when they called the intersection "McIntosh Corners." Now it is called Dundela: a straggle of white frame cottages around Smith's General Store, an abandoned outdoor hockey rink and a boarded-up red brick church. There is an historic site plaque near where the original orchard was.

Let's get it straight if we can. The Macintosh computer was invented by Apple Computer Incorporated. That makes sense. The mackintosh raincoat was invented by a Scottish man named Macintosh who, with customary Scottish humility, named his invention after himself. And the Macintosh apple was stumbled on near Dundela by John McIntosh early in the 19th century.

John McIntosh came upon his immortality by accident in the autumn of 1811, when he was chopping down the second growth of softwood trees on his farm in Matilda Township. There were a few little abandoned apple trees in the rough brush. The previous owner of the farm must have brought the seedlings with him from New York after the American Revolution.

The apples looked refreshing and John bit into one, to see what it tasted like. It had an aroma and flavour he had never known before. He liked it, so he transplanted the trees near the site of a vegetable garden he planned to put in the next Spring.

In a few years the apple from the McIntosh farm became popular among the Scottish farmers who were his neighbours. They used to call it the "Granny" apple because Grandma Hannah McIntosh was in charge of the little orchard and the vegetable garden. Later, so many people had taken small buds and branches to graft onto their own apple trees, it got to be known as the Macintosh Red.

John's son, Allan, turned the farm into a nursery for the apple and encouraged people to buy his Macintosh whips. Allan's big day was when the Macintosh Red was judged the best dessert apple in the British Empire at an agricultural exhibition in London.

The last of the original trees planted by old John survived a fire and was still bearing fruit in 1905. The next year – after at least 90 years – the old tree quit; but its name by then was part of the language.

When that original Macintosh tree died over in Dundas County, Norman Raney was six years old. Norman grew up, went to the Ontario Agricultural College in Guelph, married, bought a rolling hillside farm in Northumberland County and went into the orchard business.

One day last Spring, Mr. and Mrs. Norman Raney were sitting in the soft breeze under the butternut tree in the side yard of their home, watching the universe unfold.

Their great-granddaughter, Emily, is in the potting shed helping transplant tiny tomato seedlings. Emily's dog is learning how to nose open the makeshift hasp of the potting shed door. When the dog escapes, it does not go over so well with Emily.

Grandson Paul Chatten is over on the three-acre patch of land this side of the Simpson road. He's rototilling and fertilizing with one of the Massey 65s. It's the right day for it. There was a touch of rain over the weekend and now the soil has just the right texture and moisture. Wedged into the back of the tractor is

Rototilling young tomatoes.

Safe from wind, birds, frost.

Paul's ingenious gravity-flow fertilizer applicator – a plastic pail with a hole in the bottom. It works. The speed of the tractor and the size of the hole in the pail lets the correct amount of 15-15-15 fertilizer hit the dirt just before the rototiller teeth blend it into the soil.

Paul's father Earle is driving the other Massey 65 right behind him. Earle lays a strip of 48-inch brown plastic where Paul has rototilled. The plastic comes off a roll on the back of the tractor. Earle anchors the end of the plastic by shovelling a little dirt on it at the end of the field. Then he eases the tractor into gear. As the plastic comes off the roll, discs turn soil onto the two edges

Paul Chatten.

of the plastic so the wind can't get under the plastic and blow it away. At the other end of the row – 200 yards away – he cuts the plastic, anchors the end, turns around and starts the next strip.

When the earth gods of fertility decree, the Chattens make a row of small slashes down the centre of the plastic and plant cantaloupe seedlings. Then they put a row of hoops along the plastic strips. Over these hoops they stretch a transparent sheet of plastic and anchor it with dirt. The little cantaloupe plants in their long thin greenhouses are now safe from winds, birds and late frosts. Eighty days from today premium quality cantaloupes will be on their way to the Toronto markets.

The plastic is biodegradeable. After 90 days of sunlight the plastic simply disappears; but meanwhile it eliminates the need for boring, expensive hoeing around the seedlings. The brown plastic prevents fast-growing weeds from stealing the nourishment in the soil and choking out the little melon plants. When the plants are fully grown, their own leaves provide the protective covering that strangles weed growth.

Daughter Elizabeth is in the potting shed being patient with Emily. She has other things on her mind. This afternoon four busloads of people are coming to Pine Springs Farm as part of a tour. Each tourist gets a hearty wedge of home-made apple pie and a big glass of apple cider. The pies are cooling in Laurie's kitchen now. She will put them in the back of the new pick-up truck and drive them the 20 yards to the picnic tables set up for the tour-bus people in the orchard.

There's work to be done in the roadside stand. Coolers of fresh and smoked trout will be brought out. Apples, preserves and honey will be arranged on the shelves. New price cards will be made. The new season of roadside marketing is getting under way. Elizabeth will think of some light jokes to tell the visitors just before they get off the bus.

Granddaughter-in-law Laurie – Mrs. Paul Chatten – is in the orchard, just beyond the potting shed, pruning new Macintosh trees, trimming the small branches out of the interior of the tree so that more sunlight will reach the apples as they ripen. More sun means a redder apple. A redder apple means a better grade. A better grade means a better price. That's what it's all about.

Airbrakes hissing, doors wheezing, the first two busses pull up in front of the Pine Springs Farm roadside market. Elizabeth Chatten climbs aboard one; son Paul gets on the other. For a minute the passengers hear brief welcoming talk, full of modest self-put-downs that no one believes; but they make everyone smile.

The Homemakers Group from Knox United Church in Peterborough steps out into the cool bright day. The sunshine comes and goes as the whipped-cream clouds blow along the ridge. This outing is one of four each year for the Peterborough ladies and their husbands.

The apple blossoms are pink, translucent and frail. They fall from the branches now in the least little breeze. Like the tourists

Laurie Chatten.

from Peterborough, they are just past their peak of perfection; but no one complains.

The women line up patiently for the pie and cider. Each balances two plates and two glasses in her hands and heads for a picnic table to wait for her husband.

The men in their brightly checked jackets and slacks crowd around the glistening '29 Ford pick-up truck that Earle has restored as a promotion gimmick. The Minoltas and Pentaxes swing into action. The banter is old and familiar.

"C'mon, Elwin. Here's your chance to put your arm around somebody else's wife."

Elizabeth Chatten, roadside marketer.

"Don't go away mad. Just go away."

"Oh, I'm going on my diet tomorrow. Again."

The first bus of the new season pulls away. Elizabeth says, "I enjoy roadside marketing. I like visiting with them. They come out from Peterborough and it's a day away from the same old routine. They spend the morning shopping at the Quinte Mall, have their lunch there and come over here for the blossoms and dessert."

The other busload come from Toronto. They are younger, more affluent than the "grey power" group from Peterborough. They Indian-file into the roadside market and fan out in search of bargains. They buy everything in sight, the jams, the Cheddar, the smoked trout, last year's apples. While they sip their cider they ask Earle and Paul their urban questions. Do the bees know when it is time to pollinate? What's the difference between budding and grafting? How long is it before a tree starts to bear fruit? How come we were late for the blossoms? Is this some kind of a hobby farm or something?

Pine Springs Farm is 80 acres of apple orchard and 15 acres of vegetables on the north side of old number 2 just west of Brighton. The bus tours are a new element in the business life of the Chattens. The tours were Paul's idea. He contacted a few tour operators, just as an experiment, three years ago. It has turned out well. In the first season, 14 tours stopped at Pine Springs to see the blossoms, enjoy a piece of pie and browse in the roadside market. The apple blossom stops are incorporated into day-trip packages put together for city people in search of a touch of country.

Paul and Laurie Chatten are representative of young couples in southern Ontario who are blurring the edges between urban and rural life.

Laurie was an operating room nurse at Sunnybrook Hospital. Paul was a technical sales representative for Rohm and Haas in Toronto. Their urban future included good professional careers, children, eventually a home of their own. The ties that bind Paul to Northumberland hills must be strong. Facing a choice between salaried security in the city and the risks of partnership and ownership in the country, he and Laurie chose the country.

"Someday I knew that I would not want the city," Paul remembers. "At the time we decided, we couldn't own a detached home of our own. Real estate was that high in Toronto."

For about four years after moving to Pine Springs Farm, Laurie experienced some culture shock. The difficulty was in being accepted by the natives. That's behind her now. She smiles when she meets people who have been in Brighton for 14 years and are still awaiting acceptance.

With a Morrow computer to keep track of costs and sources of revenue, with frequent marketing trips to Toronto throughout the year, with a vice-presidency in the Ontario Fruit Growers Association, Paul blends urban sophistication with rural productivity.

"I asked myself before we came back, 'What will I do?' " The answer came quickly. He enjoys marketing and selling, even when it's difficult.

"Last year I was in Toronto selling fresh sweet corn," he recalls, "and I knew our corn was first-rate quality and the stores knew it was fresh-picked when I brought it in and I thought we should get a premium price, the same as we do with our apples. I got into a very tense situation with one of our very best apple customers in Toronto. He offered to take all our sweet corn at $3.50 a dozen. I had to explain to him that we had $3.30 invested in them before we picked them, that if we pay pickers five dollars an hour and then deliver it fresh to Toronto, at the price he offered we'd be better off to plough it under before we pick."

Marketing from the roadside is a different story. As Elizabeth explains, "You know, when families drive out from Toronto or Kingston or Ottawa, year after year, to buy their winter supplies of apples, it's not just a commercial transaction, it's more of a social event. They enjoy the drive, the scenery. They like to browse. They get time to talk about what they are buying."

Earle and Elizabeth Chatten, Pine Springs Farms.

Apple trees are like race horses. They are fragile and unpredictable when they are young. They need tender loving care and protection against weather and diseases. Like race horses, a young orchard of semi-dwarf apples takes three years of special patience before it starts to bear fruit.

In April, 1984, some Malling apple tree root stock – at $4.50

each – arrived from Holland. The Chattens planted them about 10 inches apart in the "nursery," a side hill facing south-east that gets all the spring sun there is and that is protected a little from the cold west winds.

In August, 1984, the "whips" had grown nicely and it was time to "bud" them to the apple variety they would grow up to bear – Macintosh, Spy, Delicious or Mitsu.

The miracle of budding has an Old Testament ring to it. " ... and He took one of Adam's ribs, and closed up the flesh instead thereof. And the rib, which the Lord God had taken from man, made he a woman. Bone of my bones, and flesh of my flesh. Therefore shall a man leave his father and his mother, and shall cleave unto his wife; and they shall be one flesh."

Budding is a delicate and marvellous operation that implants a small Macintosh bud in the stem of the young root stock so that the tree will mature and bear Macintosh Reds.

The operation begins with a T-shaped cut in the outer bark of the whip. You have to be gentle with a sharp knife because the outer bark is about as thin as wrapping paper. You don't want to cut into the inner core of the stem. The T-shaped cut allows you to peel back the outer bark. Then you press onto the exposed interior of the whip stem a tiny bud slip from an old Macintosh tree. The tiny stem of the Macintosh bud has been cut to nestle firmly against the inside of the root stock. Then you put back the outer bark that you peeled. You bandage up the almost invisible wound with raffia to make it airtight. The miracle has begun.

In April, 1985, the whips are cut back to just above where the buds were implanted so that all the nutrients that come up from the roots will feed into the implanted Macintosh Red bud.

In April, 1986, the whips – from four to five feet high by then – go out to their permanent place in the orchard.

During the next two years, as the trees mature, they will get "training cuts" – the pruning that determines the ultimate shape of the tree. From the arrival of the Dutch root stock to the appearance of the first few apples, it is a three-and-a-half-year process of planting, budding, transplanting, pruning, fertilizing, spraying, spraying, spraying.

When colour television first came on the air, we saw The Four Lads singing "I'll Be With You in Apple Blossom Time." They rode in a farm wagon behind a team of horses, up and down rows of apple trees that were a pink and white blizzard of colour. In those days most orchards were planted with "standard" apple trees. They were the traditional high tree with big branches drooping generously. They were planted in neat rows about 30

Spraying the semi-dwarfs.

feet apart – 34 trees to the acre. With good care – pruning, spraying, fertilizing – "standard" trees can bear fruit for 85 years.

But horticulturists cannot leave well enough alone. Centuries ago they developed miniature trees as novelties for their royal patrons. They trained fruit trees to grow like vines on espaliers.

Today the semi-dwarf apple tree is the way orchards are going. Semi-dwarfs planted just nine feet apart in rows that are 18 feet apart. The yield per tree is not going to be as great; but there are interesting economic advantages to the semi-dwarf. Ninety percent of the yield per tree is first grade and fetches a better price at the market. The yield of first-grade apples per acre is greater. The semi-dwarfs are easier to maintain. The fruit is easier to harvest. Gradually, as they reach retirement age, the old standards of Pine Springs Farm are being replaced by semi-dwarfs.

Are enough people eating an apple a day to stay out of the medical clinic? Apparently so; per capita apple consumption is increasing. Are enough teachers charmed by apples from uncertain scholars? Apparently so. Are Mom and apple pie still such evocative symbols of country virtue? Apparently so. The Chattens are increasing the yield of their orchard and increasing the quality of the apples.

Earle looks at the parking area filling up with cars. Behind him, the new storage barn is being built. With Paul and Laurie in the partnership, granddaughter Emily in the potting shed, the future is taking shape before his eyes. He smiles happily.

"We used to do this for a living. Now we're doing it for a profit."

16   Grasshopper Flats

I N THE HEART of the Northumberland hills – near Bethesda – Don Budd enjoyed the satisfactions of a well-managed dairy farm. He was good at it. His pure-bred Holsteins won best-of-show awards at the Royal Winter Fair.

For 30 years he built and maintained one of the best herds in eastern Ontario. For 30 years he milked twice a day. For 30 years he expanded and modernized as dairy-farm technology changed. There were few chances to escape from the daily demands; but

he accepted them in exchange for a life of independence, comfort, physical and mental activity and a social life in the place he had his roots.

Northumberland County is what city people mean when they say "country." The horizons are soft and distant. The land rolls comfortably and there is a wide vista of lush farmlands and generous woodlots from the crest of every hill. Concession roads disappear over the brow of the nearest hill and reappear, a little narrower, going up the next hill, and reappear again only to be lost at last in the far blue haze. Villages with clusters of old willows draped over the mill pond, with church steeples and white-fronted general stores, send age-old messages of tranquility and security. The barns with their silos and the farmhouses at the end of tree-lined lanes are the stuff of real and imaginary childhood memories.

It is this landscape – silent, green, spacious, productive, bucolic, eternal, stable – that seduces city people into thinking about "alternative" lifestyles, about "going back to our roots," about the risks their search might mean.

A few years ago Don Budd released himself from dairy-farm life. He sold the farm, the cows, the heifers, the milk quota and went into another line of business. This one has physical and intellectual demands, but of an entirely different kind.

Grasshopper Flats is a training track for harness horses on Racetrack Road just west of Baltimore, Ontario. That is not the track's official name. It has no official name. The owners and drivers

Northumberland County.

Back stretch, Grasshopper Flats.

who use the track have gotten into the habit of calling it Grass-hopper Flats, to poke light fun at Woodbine, Greenwood, Hia-leah, Churchill Downs.

Grasshopper Flats is a loosely organized cooperative. Owner/trainers use the 16 stalls on a first-come, first-served basis. Each pays a small amount each year for track maintenance. It is an ideal set-up for custodians of the dream who don't have unlimited cash.

The track is a half-mile oval that was ditched six years ago and surfaced with a hundred tons of "stone dust" – fine stone chips from Harndon and King's gravel pit just down the road. Fresh stone dust was spread on it last year. It is a horseman's track. The cement block stables are utilitarian. The horsemen use a rickety judges' stand as the starting point when they are timing their horses. There is no parking lot, no grandstand, no spectators.

Drive north on Racetrack Road and watch carefully because the track is behind a row of trees. Leave your car in the shallow ditch. From the infield of the track, there is an unobstructed view of the Great Pine Ridge in the north. High drumlins planted in oats, barley and alfalfa unfold down to the edge of the track. Birch trees and groves of maple, ironwood and cedar cluster wherever you look. A few black horses kick up their heels in a wooden corral in the infield.

Tucked in beside Grasshopper Flats' training track is the model horse farm of Mr. and Mrs. Don Budd. Birch and cedar trees shelter the bungalow from the road. There is a small vegetable garden behind the house. Two freshly painted red barns glow cheerfully in the June sunlight. Beside the barn on an easy slope, a field rolls down to a woodlot. Don lets himself through the gate, closes it behind him and stands on the slope, whistling a chirping sound. He waits.

The horseman is non-committal, fatalistic, living inside himself, cautious. The dream he dreams is a simple one: to own a foal, take it carefully up to its second birthday when it qualifies, and then send it out to win the first breeders' stake it enters. The dream is a persistent phantom in his mind, haunting him as he cares for a just-broken colt or a four-year-old pacer that hasn't raced yet because of recurring tendon problems. The horses are fragile, vulnerable, and complex. So are the dreams.

The dream doesn't come true very often, but the horses come close often enough to keep the dream alive. The obstacles are subtle, nagging little complications that happen to a horse's feet, tendons, muscles, nervous system, appetite and metabolism.

Ears pricked forward, walking sedately, a black brood mare comes up from the bottom of the field that is hidden from the gate. The pricking ears appear first, then the nodding head, the arched neck, the rippling shoulder muscles and finally the swishing tail.

Beside her, behind her, in front of her, the 12-day-old foal without a name trots and makes its miniature bucks, nuzzling her udder, rubbing against her legs, arching its neck.

Mare and foal pose and preen themselves. The aspen leaves shiver in the breeze. When the mare is in profile, the foal is in profile. When she drops her head to graze, he does too. When

Twelve-day-old newcomer on Budd Farm.

she walks cautiously away from Don, because his is only a social call, the foal's tiny hooves pound the grass with precocious authority.

The foal's legs, like those of all newborn horses, are out of proportion to the rest of the body. Here is where the dream begins. The foal's neck will grow and in a year the proportion of the head to the neck will remind you of Northern Dancer. The body will take on a graceful relation to the legs. The colt will take to the halter easily, will grow accustomed to pulling the Brodeur training cart 'round and 'round Grasshopper Flats, day in, day out. Later, in the first easy trots against the clock, the colt will come home in two minutes and fifty-five seconds. Then the training begins.

Every morning the trainer will hold the colt to a prancing walk as they go to the far end of the track. They will turn around in a slow moment of gathering expectation. Slowly the trainer will let the colt increase its speed so that, when they reach the judges' stand, horse, sulky and rider are going at the same speed as they would in a regular race behind the mobile starting gate.

The colt's legs reach far forward. The driver holds him at a steady speed. He must not let the colt burn itself out in an uncontrolled dash around the track. It doesn't take much restraint on the bit. The colt's mouth is soft now and responds easily to the pressure on the hard rubber bit.

Don Budd and Everett Adams, another owner, stand by Ev's pickup truck near the stables and watch as a colt completes the two

Everett Adams hoses down horse after morning workout.

Seven feet off the ground.

laps around Grasshopper Flats. The driver brings the panting colt into the stable area.

"What'd you get?"

"Fifty-seven."

"I made it fifty-six. That's about right." Nobody ever says "two minutes and fifty-six seconds." The "two minutes" is taken for granted.

Everett throws a blanket over the colt's back and pins it in front under the neck. The colt stands and "blows" – gets its breath back so its flanks no longer heave – for 10 or 15 minutes.

Then the driver takes the colt out to the track again for another two laps, this time slightly faster than the first: two minutes and thirty-nine seconds for the mile. Again the horse rests and then it is taken back for the third and last turn of the day around the track. The time is two minutes and twenty-six seconds.

As the weeks go by, the colt will get its time for the mile down to 2:15, 2:13, 2:11. It will take less time to "blow," to be ready for the next heat. Its body will thin out and it will get a

gaunt, race-ready look. The day comes at last, if all goes well, when the colt will do the mile comfortably in 2:10, 2:09. It's time to qualify him.

Qualifying the colt means taking it to the Peterborough track where official timers can clock him. The colt has to do the mile in 2:10 or better before it can be entered in its first race.

Back at the Budd barn, Don leads "Pod" into the shower stall. "Pod" is a five-year-old chestnut mare that hasn't raced yet. She has been working out all this spring again, gradually losing weight. Don got her when she was a year old, as collateral on a loan he made to her owner. The owner died before the debt was paid off, so "Pod" moved in. She has had tendon trouble, but every spring she is entered into the training program with the hope that this will be the year without problems.

The Budd stable is meticulous. Harness is hung painstakingly. The passageway between the box stalls is covered with rubber matting. The box stalls are spacious and carefully constructed. Everything is in its place. It looks like it was designed by someone with a businesslike approach to racing.

All the horses have been exercised, washed down, fed and watered. There is a healthy and perky new foal in the field. "We'll have to think of a name." The weather has finally changed for the better. Three of the Budd horses have been doing pretty well at Greenwood this week.

The dream is stronger than ever.

The Selby Farm, Newcastle.

17 God's Big Acre

THE LITTLE CORN PLANTS shimmer delicately in the breeze off the lake. The Currellys unhook a tank-trailer of 20% nitrogen and leave it parked beside the Case and sprayer. Steve Selby leaves the Cardin sweater on the seat of the pick-up with the BEEF licence plate and sets to work mixing the nitrogen with an herbicide in the spray tanks. Soon Steve and the rig are enveloped in a cloud of clay-coloured dust as they straddle the long parallel rows, back and forth, back and forth, until the 90 acres have been treated. You can feel the familiar urgency of Spring planting time. The number of growing days is limited.

This is the corn that fattens the cattle that go to market, where they become thick sirloins to go with the beer in Gordy's backyard, chateaubriands for two on the old expense account and the Big Macs, Burger Kings and Harveys in their zillions. Food is the business of 401 country. Ontario has more farms than any other province – 80,000 of them – and half raise beef cattle, dairy cattle and pigs. Most of them are within a hoot and a holler of the highway.

All cows eat grass.

Beef portrait.

Steve and his father, Newt Selby, run a short-keep feed lot near Newcastle. They ship more than 1,600 cattle to market every year. They grow everything the animals eat on the seven farms they own and lease.

The beef they fatten comes from Alberta. Caramel-coloured cross-breeds – Charolais mixed with Herefords – weigh in at 800 pounds when they arrive and go to market weighing eleven or twelve hundred pounds.

There is a calculated circularity here on God's big acre. The 90 acres of corn being sprayed by Steve this morning will be combined in the Fall and blown into one of the five silos. Then the kernels will be crushed and mixed with haylage, whole plant silage and supplements in the Ensilmixer – a truck-size Cuisinart which delivers it to the barn-long feeding troughs in front of the cattle. The cattle sleep, drink and eat in two vast pens that have slatted floors so that the cattle excrement is squished down into the basement, which is a holding tank. Twice a year this reservoir of nutrition is pumped out and sprayed back onto the fields to feed the tiny corn plants that will grow up to become ensilage for more cross-breeds from Alberta.

Just like dairy farmers, beef farmers don't watch television

Feeding the cross-breeds with a truck-size Cuisinart.

the way mere mortals do. If everyone should suddenly turn deaf to the splendid sizzle of Harvey's hamburger patty and blind to the wholesome Burger King lifestyle, then the demand for beef will drop, prices will drop and it won't be worth the effort to fatten cattle for a living. And why must McDonald's run so many commercials for chicken McNuggets?

Newt Selby, Newcastle.

WARNING
INSTALL TRANSPORT LOCK
BEFORE WORKING UNDER MACHINE
LOCK PREVENTS MACHINE FROM
FALLING DOWN ON YOU
FAILURE TO HEED CAN RESULT IN
DEATH OR SERIOUS INJURY

The warning stickers were strident yellow when they came from the implement dealer's, but now, after only a few years, finely crushed plant dust and clay have put a film of green-grey over them. The risks remain. The planting season is short. So is the haying season. Everything happens in high-speed bursts.

Newt unhooks his Deere from the Gehl swather and switches over to the harvester that picks up the swath of hay, chops it up and blows it into the trailing Jiffy Hydump wagon. When the Hydump is full it is taken to a great orange clam dumper that directs the hay into the silo filler.

If Newt looks north towards the Great Pine Ridge he can see his other feed lot, where 500 steers rest in Olympian detachment, shaded from the sun by big old basswoods. When he looks in

front of the house he sees a 40-acre patch of hay that should be taken off tomorrow and the field ploughed and cultivated and put into corn on the next day. That would be an around-the-clock gamble for a couple of days. It would work if the rain came right.

Lunch? Hah! A bologna sandwich in the pick-up on the way into town.

"I've got to go in and see the bank manager. I've never owed so much money in all my life."

Walls for the Tunnel

E VERYBODY LIES about how close they are to Toronto.

"I don't use the 401. I take the dayliner from Kingston, read a book, and I'm there in an hour and a half."

"From Port Hope? The 401 gets you in to good old T.O. in no time. An hour tops."

"I take a truckload of apples in three times a week. I can do Trenton to downtown in under two hours."

"Forty-five minutes to the city hall from the Liberty street exit ramp."

"The 401, yeah, keeps you close to Toronto, know what I mean?"

"C'mon, I can do from Kitchener to Maple Leaf Gardens in fifty minutes."

Two and a quarter million people are in Toronto and don't have to lie. Two and a quarter million more people outside Toronto need to feel attached to the city-state that nourishes them, with the trivia, celebrities, news and top 40 on radio; the

Bowmanville slow-ball league.

television shows you can't get from Rochester or Buffalo; the provincial politics from Queen's Park, where Bay Street and the shit-kickers get along just to stay in power.

401 country used to be loyal old Ontario clinging feebly to a rural nostalgia, to the deep-etched myth of the family farm. Not any more. The exit ramps that restrict the urban man's pursuit of his wilful rustic dreams are also the ramps that liberate the

country people's isolation from the city-state.

Now 401 country is a contemporary myth where nostalgia is kept in its place (in country music and the local museum); where food is grown and bred and marketed for unashamed profit; where self-confident individualism is the stabilizer in a changing society, where old antagonisms are being washed away in second thoughts. It is no longer the old and uneasy liaison of farmers and labour.

Today's question is, "Who shall represent us, the auto workers because they want to? Or the teamsters because they can refuse to unload the foreign ships that carry our competitors' cheaper products?"

The deep-etched myth of the family farm.

It is not all pâté de foie gras and Niagara champagne. Country people never really discovered how valuable their space was until the salaried aristocracy from the city came out in search of second homes, summer homes, hobby farms, development land. When city people buy the house or farm next door and become tax-payers and begin to take an interest in local affairs by running for township council, there begins a troubled questioning.

The man from Eldorado Refining asks, "What kind of a town do you want Port Hope to be? An old folks' home? Or a growing industrial centre?"

There is no easy answer. For generations the sign at the town limits of Port Hope said, "Port Hope – the town that radiates friendliness." That was in the dear dead days when radium was the miraculous friendly ally of hospitals treating cancer patients. Now the activist newcomers in Port Hope struggle for stricter controls on the handling of nuclear products and nuclear wastes. Old-timers in Port Hope who have depended on Eldorado for jobs and who have worn the radiation detector tags all these years don't see the danger in quite the same way. The jobs haven't changed much since the beginning of Eldorado; why have the risks? There is no easy answer.

Vintage Mustang.

401 country fades out of existence as you approach Toronto from the east. The four-lane highway becomes six lanes, then 12 lanes. Country disappears when you enter Oshawa. Here begin the walls that cut off the all-night sound of 401 traffic from the new subdivisions crowding its shoulders. The high, monotonous barricades make prisoners of the people in the subdivisions and blindfold the traveller as he gives himself to the mega-city.

These sound-dampening walls represent logical progress for the highway because the limited number of exit ramps and the bland curves and gentle hills between the cities already make it a tunnel without walls. The next logical step will be to extend the 12-foot walls along the full length of the highway and then put a roof over it.

Vintage horns and lights.

The nostalgia business is big behind those walls at Oshawa. The Canadian Automobile Museum is there on Simcoe Street. The place of honour in the museum is reserved for the 1911 McLaughlin touring car because the McLaughlin family came from a farm just up the road. The McLaughlins were like the Tudhopes, the Harrises, the Cockshutts, the Fleurys, the Andersons, the Masseys – local sleigh, buggy and implement tycoons who got in on the ground floor of the internal combustion engine revolution.

The McLaughlin sits there in its high and mighty brass-trimmed majesty, with all the sensible head room, leg room, hip room that have, little by little, year by year, been designed out of the cars we drive. Where Grandpa Condie used to step grandly up on the running board, then through the wide door to preside on the buttoned leather front seat behind the wheel, we bend over to open the door, get into a careful crouch, step over the sill and insinuate ourselves into the narrow bucket seat that is ergon-

1911 McLaughlin.

omically fashioned to keep us locked to the wheel and the instrument panel and to provoke aching lower back muscles after a couple of hours on the road.

Mosport race track is only 25 years old; but it has already become a "you-should-have-been-here-yesterday" place.

Mosport is a mammoth cathedral without a roof where pilgrims come two or three times a year to worship the noise, speed and durability of machine-and-driver tempting luck in death's neighbourhood. (Keep your eye on the crash wagon.)

Mosport is a winding track on the south flank of the Great Pine Ridge. It stands empty for most of the year. In its salad days it was on the Grand Prix Formula One circuit. Not any more. Apparently Canada can have just one Grand Prix event and it happens in Montreal.

Everything a Chevy driver must not do is done at Mosport. Race cars and motor bikes lunge far past the 100-km/h highway speed limits. Well-advertised rubber melts off bald and shrieking tires on the serpentine track. Souped-up fuels give unmuffled engines an unabashed flatulence. Race drivers tailgate, cut in,

Vintage Corvette.

and pass on the right on the outshoot of a curve.

Race day at Mosport is a sun-burning ceremony. You wait in traffic line-ups to get in; sit on plank pews, exposed to the weather, and see only a small part of the race track; stand in line for toilets and hamburgers; depend on the Player's infield sign to tell you what's really going on, and at last, long after dusk, crawl slowly out the gates towards home.

It all began in the early '60s when Albert Hill, a well-known apple grower in Durham County, sold the eroded side hill to the race promoters. In its early years the name of champion race driver Sterling Moss was associated with Mosport. The track had a reputation for British pluck and daring. But back then, the traffic jams, the boozy gate crashers, bonfires in the middle of the track in the middle of the night, the guard dogs around the perimeter, gave Mosport a darker reputation for hooliganism.

Gradually the promoters learned about crowd control. Sponsors and sports writers turned out. Mosport for a few years was part of the international circuit of Grand Prix races, for drivers accumulating points for the world championship. Racing fans

Banners scream unheard along the Great Pine Ridge.

spoke of Brands Hatch, Mosport, and Watkins Glen in the same breath.

The sponsors of racing at Mosport paint their escutcheons in blazing primary colours beside the finish line. Winners are blessed and losers forgiven in a stuttering cacophony of Castrol XLR, Yamaha, Champion, Bose, Honda, Rothman's, Porsche, Pepsi, Country Time, Pulsar, Burger King, Monroe, Walker, Player's,

Uniroyal, Canadian Tire, Michelin, Honda, Goodyear, "This Bud's For You." A winning driver – clutching the checkered flag, a silver trophy and a pretty girl – is paraded before the pilgrims, who are secretly disappointed because the crash truck never saw any action.

But for most of the year, the roofless cathedral is deserted. The banners of the sponsoring high priests scream unheard along the Great Pine Ridge. Next year there will be another cavalcade of hopeful pilgrims who come to wait for a tire to blow, a guard rail to crumble, a race car to leap off its wide wheels, a driver to be helicoptered out of the charred metal and away to intensive care.

19 *One Ambiguous Cat*

401 COUNTRY DISAPPEARED in the eastern suburbs and I did not know where I had been until I came face to face with Kivali, the white Bengal tiger in the Metro Toronto Zoo. We were both made to feel secure by the mesh of steel that separated us – she in her perfect welfare state, I in my imperfect world where drab Good battles seductive Evil, in the hope that we will survive for a little while before humanity is the last great endangered species.

Oh, that Kivali – padding indifferently from one preening place to another in the summer holiday sun – she is one ambiguous cat.

She is evil.

In the heyday of her species, Bengal tigers had a taste for people. They terrorized villages for generations and carried off their human victims by the thousands.

She is charismatic.

Her genealogy goes back to the ghost tiger in the Indian jungle that turned the natives' terror into fearful worship. The white tiger was a genetic improbability so rare the natives believed it had unnatural powers. They had no choice but to acknowledge the ghost tiger as master of their lives and, in their fear, embrace the cult of tiger worship; but that didn't tame the tiger's violence. Professional tiger killers were called on and the tiger became extinct in its native habitat.

She is doubly charismatic.

No longer endangered, because the white tiger now survives comfortably in zoos around the world, Kivali is the super-star of the rising number of species who can survive only in artificial habitats. She still attracts pilgrims by the thousands.

Kivali.

Those who don't know the awful truth about Kivali – and we are in the majority – think of her as a distant cousin of the bleached marmalade cat on the front porch.

But the evil white tiger haunted a passenger on the Amherst Island ferry, who talked of the Pickering nuclear plant up the lake shore. It doesn't need a mountain of coal or supertankers of oil to run it, he said. Instead, Pickering hums along on the invisible nuclear magic embedded in a few armloads of rods hidden in the colander.

"I don't trust what I can't see," the passenger complained. "A crazy man coming at me with a knife, I know what I'm in for; but that nuclear. Turn it loose and you can't get your hands on it."

Then there was the soft-spoken bird-watcher from Port Hope who carefully counts the buffle-head ducks every Spring as his part in an annual measurement of the bird's survival. His neigh-

"... not generating because oil costs too much."

bours tell him he should be more concerned about the radiation count at Eldorado Refining, where he has worked for 20 years. Yet he's worn his radiation detector card all those years and it never went "tilt" on the way through the scanner. He couldn't see any white tiger lurking in the nuclear bushes; but there is one threatening the birds in his binoculars and he wants to stop it.

Usually the white tiger that needs to be caged began in the minds of thoughtless men a long time ago. Today, thoughtful men hope they are not too late on too cold a spoor.

Generations of over-fishing had made the trout as near-extinct as the Bengal tiger, so man made a little peace with the environment and built a fish ladder that climbs the Ganaraska a hundred feet away from the 401. Handsome trout in the thousands somehow will themselves up the concrete risers into the still waters of the Ganaraska valley, where they spawn and die and their fingerlings flood back to the open waters for another chance at survival.

What was the white tiger that drove the white pelican onto the endangered list? DDT accumulating in the liver? A surfeit of man's cast-off chemicals weakening the egg shells? Compassion got the white pelican flying again after his crash-landing on the 401. There's no need for a place for him in the zoo. Yet.

And there are Bryce Rupert's turtles on the old log in the swamp. Before man came along they could survive the skunks and herons of their youth; but man's Ark has sprung too many intellectual leaks. Acid rain is eating the snails. The road-builder is draining all the marshland dry. Get the turtle pavilion ready.

All is not gloom in this world of genetic uncertainty. Sometimes the white tiger turns into a benign little pussycat.

There is the astonishing search for the perfect Holstein cow – a genetic numbers game being scrolled out in the breeders' computers. What if they find her? Will there be an air-conditioned pen at the zoo where all can come to see perfection? Or is she a black and white ghost – a genetic freak lurking in the underbrush of some forgotten breeder's record books?

Back at Grasshopper Flats the dreamers and believers consult their form charts in search of the healthy, firm-boned colt that will defy the white tiger of tendonitis and come home in 1:52 in its first breeders' stake race.

What about the doctor in Cobourg who bought abandoned farms north of town, where the sand was perfect for growing tobacco? Now that the white tiger of lung cancer has been identified, does he warn his patients not to smoke? Or does he hope to sell the tobacco to less-developed countries where the people don't have a well-developed fear of cancer. Yet.

The voyage of discovery is finished. The discovery is the ambiguous white tiger that is in us and stalks all of us.

ON THE WAY TO THE MUSEUM

1   "Ride on, Ride on in Majesty"

Listen to the word "truck." It has an unequivocally blue-collar sound to it. It explodes down out of your mouth with the same shock as the old, familiar obscenity for sexual intercourse. There is no doubt what a truck is, what trucking is.

But the trucker, especially the highway truck driver, is too complex to be reduced to a phrase. He is the cowboy, the drifter, the Indian scout, the harvester following the ripening wheat from south to north, Charles Lindbergh in *The Spirit of St. Louis*, Frances Chichester sailing around the world alone. He is the itinerant Australian sheep shearer, the stud horse man, the bush pilot, the homeless gypsy moving from town to town.

He drives most of his miles by night. Darkness isolates him. A folklore of melancholy has grown up around the way he makes his living; but he has developed his own tactics to fight it off.

The 401 truck driver is the aristocrat of the asphalt. Between Montreal and Windsor there are gas stations, motels, specialized repair and installation services, restaurants and dealerships which do not especially welcome the general public as customers because they are too busy serving just the needs of the highway truck driver. From midnight to noon, the four-lane expressway belongs to him. He drives at least 100,000 miles a year.

He is a member of a closely-knit fraternity that gets together in random meetings at all-night restaurants every hundred miles or so. He keeps in touch with other drivers with his CB radio. He leaves it on for the entire trip so he can hear the unexpected along the night expressway. He is courted aggressively for his disposable income by advertising in all-night radio-programs and monthly newspapers produced expressly for him.

Once a year, the 401 drivers come together for a dinner and dance. There is no formal association to organize the affair. Last year, a driver for Glengarry Transport was responsible and turned it into a kind of Oscar awards night for the drivers. Nobody is exactly sure when or where it will be this year; but it will happen and the awards will be as funny as the dubious achievements that win them.

Pat Hanley drives for Kingsway Transport out of Dorval. After he finished Holy Cross and Montreal High Schools, Pat joined the Army. Seven years later he got his discharge and went back into civilian life with army papers to show he was a truck-driving specialist. He has been driving for Kingsway for 21 years, mostly on city pick-up and delivery. Four years ago he started stand-by driving – substituting for highway drivers with more seniority – on weekends and holidays. Last year he got into the regular highway rotation. Pat is married and the Hanleys have three children.

Marcel Delisle drives for Kingsway out of the Windsor terminal. He is a quarter-century man at Kingsway and clocked

The John Lougheed Family.

his two-millionth mile of accident-free driving in 1985. Marcel is married and the Delisles have four children.

John Lougheed's runs start at the Kingsway terminal in Toronto's west end. John learned tractor-trailer driving at a special course given by the Toronto Board of Education. He put in the usual apprenticeship as a city pick-up and delivery driver. He is married and the Lougheeds have three children.

Pat, Marcel and John were the drivers of tractor number 51404 when it did a routine round trip through 401 country – the busiest 828 kilometres in Canada.

The humidity was awful all day Monday. It felt like we were building up to a big storm. Pat Hanley was out back, mowing the lawn of his Greenfield Park home. Bev was in the kitchen preparing her spaghetti-and-meatballs recipe for dinner. The three Hanley children were off somewhere, probably swimming in one of the neighbours' pools.

When the phone rang a little after five, Bev knew before she picked it up that it would be the dispatcher, wanting Pat.

"It's for you, Pat."

There was a quiet, matter-of-fact exchange on the phone. Bev knew that Pat would be on his way sometime after seven o'clock that evening.

The dispatcher gave Pat his choice of a run to New York or Toronto. New York meant more money of course, but then there was the long layover. Besides, the weather forecast didn't sound that great. If it were going to rain, Toronto would be the better run. The same choice had been given to Hector Joubinville just a few minutes earlier but Hector had a doctor's appointment the next day. The dispatcher went down the list.

The truck drivers – in order of their seniority – are given just two hours' notice of their next run by this phone call. It's the sort of thing that can be real hard on family life sometimes.

At the terminal in Dorval, dock foreman Fernand Lemay – a 33-year man – watches carefully as the trailers are loaded. It's a 98-door terminal where fork-lifts and hand dollies move the freight from this door to that.

During the day, the city p. and d. trucks brought in brake units for Kenworth trucks, Flex hair shampoo, huge rolls of suit fabrics from Italy, Westinghouse power switching equipment, a rotor and shaft going to Alcan in Arvida, plastic extrusions, refrigeration equipment, heavy oil drilling equipment for Pan-arctic Oils (via St. John's, Newfoundland), pipeline valves, rolls of broadloom and a shipment of cigarettes going back to the factory.

A fork-lift slides up beside Fernand Lemay's office. The operator in a chic blue cap is the lean, swarthy golf champion of Kingsway, Robert Pilon. Lemay smiles a brief smile of conspiracy and says, "He doesn't talk very much."

Pilon talks non-stop in English and in French, to the foreman, to himself, to the other fork-lift operators, to the packers, to the night air. "I just love this job. I wouldn't change the night shift here for anything. After this I can go home to Laval, sleep until noon, get up, have a good breakfast, go out for a round of golf. It's a great life." His eyes flash and he jockeys the fork-lift like a golf cart between the sixteenth green and the seventeenth tee and goes off in search of Charlie Brown encyclopaedias, Volvo parts and helicopter parts for one of the trucks going to Toronto tonight.

At a quarter to eight a steady rain is greasing up the roads. Distant forks of lightning are a prelude to a different kind of night for driving. Two Ford 9000s crouch in the darkness ready to go. Both have been hitched to 45-foot trailers loaded for Toronto.

Pat Hanley leaves the dispatcher's office and picks up his briefcase, the overnight bag, the two aerials and the box with his CB and AM radios. He runs across the tarmac, dodging puddles, and climbs up into the cab of 51404. He bolts the CB aerial onto the rear-view mirror bracket. He clamps the AM aerial on the door window. He runs the aerial cables to the box and straps the box securely under the dash. He takes a tachograph card out of his briefcase, signs it and locks it under the tachometer in the dash. He cannot take the tachograph out until he has completed the run. It's a tough business. He puts the time and mileage onto his log sheet, zips up the meticulous briefcase and he's ready to go.

Directly behind him, in 51416, Jean-Guy Poirier has gone through the same procedure as Pat – the aerials, the tachograph, the log book. Both engines jump into life. Both AM radios fill the cabs with music. Pat flicks his lights and the two rigs ease out onto Cote de Liesse which takes them down to Quebec highway 20.

They will stay close to each other on the run to Toronto. Truck drivers are compulsive about safety. Knowing there is another company driver close by is reassuring. Pat's load is bulky but not particularly heavy. Jean-Guy's load is close to the maximum weight so his momentum will put him ahead of Pat when they reach the 100 km/h limit on the open road.

Pat sits high on an air-cushioned seat that absorbs the steady pounding of the rig. Without the $450 seat, Pat's body would be straining against the rhythmic lurching as the tractor and trailer thrust against each other with each bump in the road.

Highway 20 has a series of stoplights between Cote de Liesse and the Ontario border. The air brakes hiss and wheeze at each one. Pat gears down for the lights and gears up after the green. The truck is slow and deliberate in the suburban traffic. Job would have made a good highway driver.

By now the electrons and decibels of God are putting on a spectacular *son et lumière* show. Far ahead to the right, the red sun is making a hazy exit. On both sides of the truck, lightning in massive queen-size sheets floods the passing landscape in strobic blazes of glory. Far ahead to the left, over the river, lightning smothered inside dark clouds bumps and murmurs. A hundred and fifty miles straight up, the space shuttle Challenger is videotaping the top of the electrical storm. It'll be on the TV news tomorrow night when Pat gets back to Greenfield Park.

The two Kingsway rigs are rolling now. The governor on Pat's engine prevents the truck from going faster than 100 km/h; but Pat keeps an eye on the speedometer anyway. Sometimes on a downhill pull the needle can creep up past 105 or 110. As they cross the border onto Ontario's highway 401, they join the caravan of eighteen-wheelers – by the dozen, by the hundreds – doing a steady 99 to 101 km/h in the dark wet tunnel of night. Random lightning sheets are as bright as the sun and tough on radio reception. The west-bound inspection station light is flashing. The two rigs ease over onto the exit ramp. They are waved through without having to pass over the weigh scales.

A noisy isolation closes in around Pat. The AM radio fills the cab with "good music." The CB radio squawks into life now and then. Voices tell the eastbound drivers the weigh station is open tonight. The electrical storm outside rips the sound of the two radios into shreds. The sun sets and is replaced in the southern sky by a full moon that outlines the edges of the storm clouds moving slowly north.

The rigs pull into the Texaco station at Morrisburg. They've been on the road now for just over an hour and a half. Pat walks slowly around the trailer, kicking every tire, laying a hand on each one. When the driver kicks the tire he listens for a taut *boink* that tells him the air pressure is okay. He can't tell just by looking at the tire because there are two of them, side by

side. One could be without air yet look full, while the other holds up twice as much of the axle weight as it should. He checks to see whether any tires are running hot. He pays particular attention to the tires on the trailer because they are recapped tractor tires. In certain hot-weather conditions the rough, hot highway surface can peel the heated cap off a tire and fling it in tatters onto the shoulder. Kingsway drivers do a tire inspection like this every hundred miles. At the end of the run the tachograph will show the exact time and mileage of each inspection.

In the restaurant, Pat and Jean-Guy join drivers from other transport companies. Pat lights up a Mark Ten. He listens more than he talks.

One driver who owns his own tractor decides he'll crawl into his sleeper and wait for the storm to pass through.

"When you drive you drive. When you sleep you sleep. And no fooling around in Chicago. That's my motto."

At the next table an owner-driver wearing a Led Zeppelin T-shirt has just learned the eastbound weigh station is open tonight.

"Why does that bother him?"

"You weren't at the 401 drivers' party last fall, were you?"

"No."

"He's the driver that got the trophy for being caught over-weight the most times last year."

The storm was still hard at it when the rigs pulled out onto the 401 again. Between Morrisburg and Napanee there were fog patches. Hail stones drummed across the engine hood. Visibility was nothing to write home about in the rainy darkness. Oncoming lights refracted through the rain and created dazzling stars on the windshield. Pat's hands never left the wheel.

Even under ideal conditions, handling the wheel is a constant concern on the 401 because the increasing number of eighteen-wheelers over the years has put two wide, shallow grooves in the surface of the right-hand lane – grooves that sometimes shift the truck wheels up the sides and back. This sideways shifting, along with the forward lurching of the tractor-trailer, means there can be no "automatic pilot," no daydreaming, no casual cruising with an elbow cocked out the window.

It's ten to one and the storm has tapered off. The full moon in the clear southern sky rides along with the truck towards Toronto. The next stop is the Shell station near Trenton. The tarmac is packed hub-nuts to hub-nuts with big rigs with walk-in sleepers behind the cabs. The owner-drivers sleep here, waiting for morning when their customers' receiving docks will be open. There's not much room left for the driver who just wants to stop for a coffee break. Pat doesn't eat during these short stops. A couple of Mark Tens, a couple of cups of coffee and some low-key shop-talk with the other drivers put him in shape for the last leg of the trip.

Truckers don't like big-city rush hours so they try to time their arrivals and departures to avoid the jams. At three in the morning Pat passes a long line of rigs parked on the wide shoulder of the 401 near Pickering. The drivers are sleeping until five o'clock, when they will drive into Toronto before the morning rush hour. Pat rumbles across the empty 16-lane section of the

401 to 427. He goes south on 427 and curls off to Queensway Boulevard and the Kingsway terminal.

At 3:25 Pat backs the trailer to a loading door, unhooks it from tractor 51404 and drives the tractor over to the "bunkhouse," where he will sleep for at least seven hours before getting ready for the return trip to Montreal. He takes the tachograph and his log sheet into the Toronto dispatcher's office. The dispatcher now knows he will have a new driver available at 10:30 for a run to Montreal; and he has tractor 51404 available to take one of Kingsway's 2,000 trailers to another destination.

Pat Hanley takes his two radios and aerials into the bunkhouse with him. In the doorway he meets Marcel Delisle, who grumbles about having to shift his radio box and aerials out of "his" truck and into Pat's 404. Most of Marcel's driving is on the Toronto–Windsor run. Because of his seniority and his good-natured joshing with the dispatchers, most of the time he can leave his gear in an '84 Ford with a Cummins engine. Like most drivers, Marcel argues that a tractor lasts longer if it is driven by one driver only. Marcel says "his" Cummins is quieter than the Caterpillar in 404. But dispatchers have other things on their minds at four o'clock in the morning.

Marcel tops up the fuel tanks of 404, installs his aerials and goes over to the trailer shop to wait while a trailer is packed for Windsor. In the shop during the pre-dawn coffee break the conversation between Marcel Delisle and Roland Dagenais borders on character assassination and libel. It turns out they are related by marriage. Family affection, not mid-shift fatigue, brings out the insults.

Roly is a welder and trailer maintenance man. He lives in Mississauga but carries with him at all times a powerful yearning for Fort Coulanges on the Quebec side of the Ottawa river. He reminisces happily about hunting expeditions when the bears refused to fall down dead, when deer grazed peacefully behind him as he scanned the wrong underbrush with his binoculars, and when bull moose ignored the seductive sound of water dribbled from a pail in imitation of the sound of an incontinent lady moose.

After one last flurry of shafts about a general lack of height, sexual prowess and good looks, Marcel goes to hook 404 to the trailer. He brings the rig back into the trailer shop. Roly slides under and checks the brakes and tires.

Marcel heads north on 427. If highway 401 is the aorta of Canadian commerce, then 427 is its left ventricle; 427 connects the Queen Elizabeth Way to the 401. All the truck transport nourishing the golden horseshoe from Niagara to Oshawa and everywhere in between throbs 24 hours a day through the 12 lanes of 427.

The west-Toronto commuters, their freshly-shaved jaws clenched, pass on the left of Marcel, cut in suddenly and race for a narrowing slot in the passing lane. They are busy daring death to prevent them from getting to work on time.

Marcel gears up slowly and the rig curves off 427 and back onto 401 heading for Windsor. Above the ascending engine rumble, Marcel can hear a deeper, more insistent roar as airplanes, stacked over Lake Ontario, take their turns landing at Toronto's International Airport. Their flight path is a few hundred feet above him.

Gradually the highway shrinks from 12 lanes, to six, to four. Beside the Ontario Agricultural Museum, 401 country re-emerges. Tranquil fields of corn, barley and soy beans, barns and blue silos are in Marcel's peripheral vision. The city was a frantic concrete launching pad for this bucolic cruise across southwestern Ontario.

With the morning sun behind him and the needle at 100 km/h, Marcel sets his radio at CBL. Embedded in the Peter Gzowski talk show is a soap opera dealing with adultery among the nobs of Alberta fifty years ago. Marcel listens with the close attention of an addict. He will be listening tomorrow and tomorrow and tomorrow. The radio takes the place of someone to talk to in the cab. There is no seat for "someone to talk to." The "no riders" policy of trucking companies reduces the chance of a lawsuit launched by a hitch-hiker, relative or friend who might be in the truck during an accident. A seat for someone to talk to would not serve the purpose anyway because the noise level is too high. Rider and driver would have to shout at each other until they were hoarse. The CB receiver is left on channel 12 to pick up anything other drivers might have to say. The volume on CBL is high. Marcel doesn't want to lose any hanky-panky in high places because of the ear-ringing engine noise.

At the first stop on a bright and perfect summer day, the banter among the drivers is light-hearted small talk about the way they make their living: about people and situations that have to be tolerated.

"Sure, I know that long-legged whore. Well enough to call him a long-legged whore to his face. He and I go a long way back. I know everybody," Marcel says. It may be true. During his two million miles of accident-free driving, he has made 20,000 stops at gas stations, truck stops, motels, freight terminals and customers' receiving doors. He has gotten to know drivers, dispatchers and dock foremen, even the introverted ones. Some-where, sometime in all those miles he has met all the drivers whose voices he has heard on the CB.

"Down in Quebec they'd call it a *maudite crachoire* – a damned spittoon of a truck. Me, I call it a gutless piece of junk; but I guess a gutless piece of junk depends on which diesel is on what chassis."

"Cabovers? A lot of drivers don't like them because you're sitting directly above the front axle and you get every bump. I don't mind them. In a cabover you're sitting higher than any-body and you can see further ahead. That's the thing of a cabover. You can see right over the roof of a Winnebago. You need that kind of visibility with a full load behind you."

It is a western Ontario summer day: hot and clear after the weekend rain. The corn is tasselled out nicely now. It looks like it's going to be a good year. The barley is an even bleached gold and in the shifting mid-day light the bent heads undulate like the reflections in a silk Persian rug. The second-cut alfalfa is a thick tangle of green with faint touches of purple blossom. The fields of soybeans are swarthy green mats. Here and there fields of cucumbers are being harvested. Bold yellow and red plastic pails are scattered randomly between the rows, waiting for the pickers. Squint your eyes a little to diffuse the sharp edges and you are looking at a Gershon Iskowitz painting of yellow and red blobs floating in a great sea of green. Up ahead, the 401 rolls over a gentle rise and there is Jack Chambers' painting of the Woodstock exit ramp – the real thing.

The rich farmland spreads out in all directions, overflowing the windshield of the truck. It is a world where the drivers meas-ure the distance in miles, not kilometres; the fuel in gallons, not litres; the load in pounds, not kilograms. It is a world where the driver is passed from one favourite radio station to another as he moves from one broadcast area to the next. It is a world where the driver becomes attached to a certain restaurant on the route because it is the right distance from the terminal for a tire check. He gets to know the people in the restaurant and they become accustomed to his outbursts of corny affection.

"Put a hug on the bill, Marg."

Certain gas stations and fast food franchises have "lousy cof-fee and outrageous prices." Others don't have enough space for the rigs. Some are just too clumsy for a 45-foot trailer on an exit ramp with sharp turns.

West of London, Marcel pulls into a service area and lines his rig up with a row of Peterbilt, Freightliner, Kenworth, Inter-national, Western Star and Mack trucks. He climbs down and

kicks all the tires. In the restaurant he takes an order of french
fries and gravy over to the round table with the other drivers.
He douses the fries with ketchup. The drivers shake their heads
in amazement. Fifteen minutes later as he guides the rig across
the flatlands of Essex county, towards the Renaissance Tower
shining on the far horizon in Detroit, Marcel reaches for his
overnight bag, takes out a bottle of Maalox and swallows a
mouthful. After he unhitches at the Windsor terminal, he logs
out with the dispatcher. Smiling comfortably, he thinks he's
ready for a beer.

In 20 hours, tractor number 51404 with Pat Hanley driving hauled
20 tons from Montreal to Toronto, where it changed trailers and
drivers and took another 20 tons to Windsor with Marcel Delisle
at the wheel. It was one of a thousand eighteen-wheel rigs on
the 401 that day – not the prettiest, not the ugliest, not the
newest, not the oldest – with a cautious and soft-spoken highway
driver riding alone in the high cab, a noisy reliable diesel engine
out front, a CB receiver crackling for news of the road and music
from an AM radio filling the spaces of the cab.

Whether it's Pat or Marcel, the highway driver watches the traffic far ahead, the cars passing, the trucks merging into the right lane, the tail-gaters, the weavers, the cautious, the speeders. His eyes move from the rear-view mirror on the left door to the one on the right door and back again. He drives with a special courtesy for other truck drivers. When he is about to pass a truck he signals with his lights. Before he gets back into the right lane he waits for a signal from the truck behind that there is clearance enough. He works with a constant and careful awareness that he is perched on top of 40 tons of tractor, trailer and cargo. He looks at the constantly changing options far ahead. He watches the traffic behind. He drives by the book.

He drives a truck that is without nuance. In spite of all the chrome and corporate design, the tractor is a huge, snub-nosed brute. It does one thing relentlessly well: pulls big loads over long distances. There is no pretence of styling or streamlining. There is a big wide square hood over the engine because there is a big wide powerful engine under it. The cab is small because that's all the driver needs. It sits high because the driver needs the height to see where the momentum of 40 tons at 60 miles an hour is heading. There are $7,500 worth of Michelins on the tractor. They get a little precautionary affection every hundred miles.

Unlike Pat and Marcel, who drive for a transport company, many of the highway drivers own their own tractors. The driver who has chosen to be self-employed doesn't have to settle for the intrinsic brute beauty of the machine as it comes from the factory. Although he will never be able to pretend it has the low, feral beauty of a Jaguar or the autobahn authority of a Mercedes, he can enhance it with chrome accessories and murals painted on the sides. He can reveal something of his personality by his choice of the sleeper he buys and attaches to the back of the cab.

Last year at the "Show and Shine" competition in Cayuga, Mike Davidson won first prize in the "Best Truck" division for his 1980 Freightliner with its razzle-dazzle flying horse mural on the sides. The wheels, hub caps, lug nut covers, the six-foot exhaust stacks, rear bumper, mud-flap holders, front bumper, air vents and cleaners and back-up lights are all chromed. The grip handles, bumper guides, cab and sleeper trim, fuel permit plates and bug deflectors are stainless steel. The full fenders, deck plate, rear frame enclosure, six-foot storage box and fuel tanks are polished aluminum.

Mike's cab has the $450 Eldorado air seats with arm rests, twin heaters, twin roof-mounted defrost fans, heated mirrors, air-conditioning, roof spotlight, a radar detector, Sony AM/FM stereo radio with cassette deck, Cobra CB radio and a digital alarm clock.

The custom-built sleeper is an air-conditioned room eight feet by eight feet by six feet with windows in the roof. There is a walk-in closet and a half-length closet. The bed – eight feet by four feet – converts into a table and chairs for four people. A microwave oven and colour television are built in. A 4500-watt Honda generator runs everything. The walls are naugahyde. Wall-to-wall carpeting continues into the driver's cab.

When Mike pulls out of the Bauhaus Furniture yard in Toronto with his 48-foot stainless steel trailer in back, he's in charge of a 71-foot showpiece that has racked up well over a million miles so far. It is his factory, his office and his home on the road. Toronto to Seattle and back. Toronto to Portland and back. Toronto to everywhere and back. You might as well look like a million-miler. Besides, it's good for business.

There are highway romantics who say these brightly chromed and painted monsters are to metropolitan man what yesterday's covered wagons were when they brought food, tools, shelter, clothing, medicine, education to the pioneers of southern Ontario.

But when you take the 401-highway driver out of his Freightliner, he could as easily be the credit officer at the local bank branch, or a customers' man at the stockbrokers, a bureaucrat, an assistant brand manager, a certified public accountant, a Bell Canada repairman or the owner of a neighbourhood convenience store.

However, the mystique remains. They write songs about truck drivers. They don't write songs about bankers, brokers or brand managers. When the breweries want to convince you their beer is brewed expressly for attractive, free-wheeling he-men – like the one rattling around in secret in the heart of every cautious man – they put their bottle in the hands of all the young Robert Redfords and Burt Reynoldses, the evening sun glinting on the hair of their forearms as they drop lightly down from the chrome majesty of their cabs and swashbuckle their way to the nearest tavern.

The highway driver leads what looks like a hassle-free life. (Don't think about the bank payments.) He drives the length and breadth of the continent. He is the clear-eyed, resolute loner whose inner life, including the emotional complications of being away from home, of being vulnerable to other night-breathing loners, makes him the hero of adolescent dreams.

The momentum behind those thousands and thousands of eighteen-wheel rigs moving from city to city – high above the

Marcel Delisle, two million miler.

ordinary Volkswagen Rabbit crowd – began with the inexorable lurch of the early nineteenth-century Conestoga wagons that made it through swamps, across rivers, down escarpments to the rich and rolling landscape of southern Ontario.

Alone in his cab, the driver has no hierarchy or bureaucracy to bug him. He is an aristocrat in the folklore of the day. He always has a destination. He has his independence. He is free.

Night again. Time for Marcel Delisle to go back to Toronto. A waning moon hangs over his left shoulder as Marcel parks his red Ford pick-up in the yard of Kingsway's Windsor terminal. After an early dinner at home with the whole family in Amherstberg and a full evening's sleep, he is ready for the return run. In the service bay, he talks carefully of the two million safe miles he has driven, of the last few round trips between Windsor and Toronto. He is Pete Rose hustling at bat for another hit to reach the 4,192nd of his career. He is Tom Seaver pitching seven good innings to win his 300th game. Marcel's two million miles of driving remind him, somehow, of his father's 43 years as a section man for the old Temiskaming and Northern Ontario railroad up in Ansonville. Good-natured endurance.

Marcel gossips, free associates and tunes the radios in the cab as he waits for the sealed trailer which is being brought across the Ambassador Bridge from Detroit. He tells of the driver who solved his marriage problems by arranging tractor-trailer driving lessons for his wife. She passed the tests and is now her husband's second driver on regular long hauls to the west.

The radio fills the cab with sounds that play leapfrog with Marcel's memories.

"This is WCKI in Detroit and from six p.m. to midnight every Saturday night it's Motor City Country time."

"I worked on the shipping dock in Toronto for a while, but I guess I got white line fever. I missed the highway."

"This is WLW in Cincinatti. Fifty-thousand-watt voice of the American trucker. This is Bozo. Got your ears on? We're with you all night every night."

"She was the fallen·angel of Truckers' Paradise ... a big producer from Hollywood led her astray."

"Hello, Bozo, this is Crazy Casper in Buffalo. Just thought I'd let you know I'm driving for St. Johnsbury now out of the Syracuse terminal."

"Glad you called, Crazy Casper, keep in touch."

"I'm the same old me, the same old me."

"How much do you need? Not an awful lot. One thousand or two thousand up front. Just call Transportation Equipment Management Corporation."

"This professor got permission to ride in the cab with me and he had me all wired up to a galvanometer. I had wires coming off my head into his black box. He was measuring stress somehow. I wore that harness of his all the way to Montreal. Well sir, when we got to Montreal, know what this professor said? He says, 'I need a woman.' Honest to God's truth, that's what he said. 'I need a woman real bad.' The shaking and the shimmying and the humping up and down in that cab all those miles got him shook up real good. Really turned him on."

"Heaven knows we've seen the storm clouds gather."

"Kiss an angel good morning."

"Thank you, Charlie Pride. That's good advice for Big Cuddles. Sweet Baby over in Lancaster tells me she hasn't heard from Big Cuddles in months. She's just waiting beside her phone. Anybody out there gets Big Cuddles on the CB tell him to phone Sweet Baby right off. Tell him you heard it from Bozo, WLW Cincinnati, seven hundred on your dial, the voice of the American trucker."

"So help me, it's true. He was doing 65 in a 55 zone and the smokey picks him up and just trails him. Every CBer on the road for a good 16 miles keeps telling him there's a smokey on his tail, but he keeps on breaking the law. Finally the smokey pulls him over and says, 'Didn't you hear all them good buddies on your radio telling you I was right behind?' Know what he says to the smokey? He says, 'Hell, I was just so wrapped up in Bozo's show on WLW I didn't hear a damned thing.' "

Marcel hooks 404 to the sealed van and heads for Toronto. It is after midnight. Both radios are tuned up. Bozo keeps him company. As the truck gets closer to Toronto the "voice of the American trucker" begins to weaken. Remote radio stations bounce their crackling signals in on top of the fading Bozo. For a brief, static-filled moment, the sound of a southern church choir fills the cab.

"Ride on, ride on in majesty ... hark all the tribes Hosannah cry ... oh Saviour meek, pursue thy road ... crrackle ... garments strowed ... sputter crrracck ... in lowly pomp ride on to die ... bow thy meek head to mortal pain ... "

Near Kitchener there is the body of a dead deer on the eastbound shoulder. The CB radios come to life as the eastbound drivers discuss this mortality with the westbound drivers.

John Lougheed has the gaunt serenity of a pre-Civil War Abe Lincoln. In the trailer shop at Kingsway's Toronto terminal, he puts his aerials in place where Marcel's used to be. He waits for Roly Dagenais to check the brakes and tires.

Two retired drivers – both ruddy-cheeked and overweight – get up from a bench to come over and talk to John.

"What the hell kind of a truck driver are you anyway, John? Look at us. Our bellies stick out a mile. Yours curves in. What's wrong with you?"

He laughs easily. "I eat light because there's too much shaking around."

But it is no laughing matter. Truck drivers are plagued by digestive and cardiovascular problems, caused partly by the sedentary nature of the job, partly by stress, partly by atrocious eating habits on the job, partly by their lifestyle.

On average, truck drivers absorb 3,655 calories a day when all they need is 2,000. Too many calories. Too much fat. Too much salt. Not enough calcium. Not enough fibre. Not enough vitamins A and C. Not enough exercise. Too much smoking.

Eight out of 10 drivers have pot bellies or are overweight to the point of obesity. Eight out of 10 drivers have stomach problems caused by stress. Three-quarters of them don't get two hours of exercise in a week. Half of them drink and smoke. Every eighth driver has high blood pressure.

It used to be folk wisdom that truck drivers knew where all the good highway restaurants were. Whenever you saw a roadside restaurant surrounded by dozens of big rigs, that's where the great meals were. It was wrong back then and it's still wrong. Truck-stop restaurant meals are expensive and overloaded with calories to give the driver the quick hit of sugar that will keep him alert for another hundred miles.

John (with the concave belly) got the call from the dispatcher at 4:30 in the morning. The sealed van from Detroit would be ready to go to Montreal at 6:30. He liked that. He liked the early morning call.

"I prefer driving days so I can watch the scenery go by."

He gets out of Toronto before the morning rush hour starts and drives into a steady rain.

"They say good highway drivers have diesel fuel for blood. I don't know about that. I do think, though, I get to spend more time with my family than people with regular nine-to-five jobs."

John has thought long and hard about owning his own tractor. The trend in the industry seems to be away from company drivers and towards more brokers. (Brokers are drivers who own their tractors and have exclusive contracts with transport companies.) Most of the pros and cons are clear in his mind. As a company driver with some seniority he doesn't have to worry about the financing, maintenance, fuel or insurance on the trucks he drives. As a broker he would become eligible for the longer and better-paying hauls like Toronto to Winnipeg, Toronto to Calgary or into the United States. As a broker he could safely drive enough miles in each month to pay off the loan on the tractor in four years; but the inner dialogue is full of ifs and buts and what-ifs. A new set of tires would cost $7,500. Just to say "Fill 'er up" costs $400. He knows most of the arithmetic of ownership. The piece he is missing is a believable forecast of his income. He has to guess how much he would be able to keep for himself: from $20,000 up to $65,000 a year.

He runs over the numbers again. From $2,000 to $3,600 a month to finance the purchase of the truck; $3,200 for 1,600 gallons of fuel a month; $333 a month for licence plates; $175 a month for insurance – but they say that's going to go through the roof. That adds up to at least $5,750 in expenses every month. And we haven't paid for any maintenance. Typical monthly income for brokers – based on an average payment of $1 a mile

"He drives into a steady rain."

– is about $8,000. Optimistically that leaves a take-home pay of $2,250 a month or $27,000 a year.

He is under no pressure to buy his own tractor; but if it ever comes to that, he knows the one he will buy. It is a deluxe R-model Mack with a 50-inch walk-in bunk and a 350-horsepower engine.

"Built like a Mack truck" is the insult all teenagers have used

since the beginning of time to describe the girl who looks wider than she is tall, with broad shoulders, thick thighs and a personality to match. The deluxe R has that kind of boxy charm. The walk-in bunk means just that. You can pull the Mack off to the shoulder, leave the running lights on, turn around in the driver's seat and walk into a bedroom, where you sleep for an hour or two or flake out for eight hours. The bunk lets you get in more safe driving hours in 24.

"I don't know. When you've got those finance payments on your mind, do you risk your own life by worrying about meeting the payments and maybe driving more miles in a day than you should?"

For his last tire check before Dorval, he stops at Lancaster and buys a fresh fish roll from the chip wagon on the main street. He eats the fish and throws away the roll.

"That's good. That tastes like fish."

As he gears the rig up to 100 km/h on the straight run across the Lancaster flats into Quebec, an Olds slips past him. The driver is reading a road map spread across the steering wheel. John shakes his head.

"Read a book. Peel an orange. Drink pop. Snuggle. Fondle. Keep a dog on the lap. It's amazing. Anything they do parked they'll do while they're driving. Anything."

That night, back in Windsor, Marcel Delisle's son, Patrick, comes home from a ball game at Tiger Stadium with a present for his father. It's a baseball cap with a slogan across the front:

"Now that I understand women, I love my truck."

2   Men with White Foreheads

I
T WAS NO SKIN OFF OUR NOSES when the stock market crashed because nobody around here knew much about stocks and bonds. Lord's sake, we were small potatoes. We didn't know we were in the middle of a depression until it was over. What *we* saw was things changing too fast and we were torn apart, I tell you.

Where were we going to find a hired man any more who'd work hard for $20 a month plus room and board? A young guy could go over to Detroit and get a job on the Ford line sandpapering wooden wheel spokes, and make more money in two days than we could pay him for a month. Even if you owned a hundred acres clear and free you couldn't make that kind of money farming.

The boys who went out west for the wheat harvest came home for Christmas (if they came back at all) and brought snapshots of eight-furrow gang plows pulled by teams of 18 horses; gasoline tractors with eight-foot steel wheels pulling four binders hitched together. A single field of wheat out there was bigger than our whole farm down here. That made us feel kind of puny and jealous, I guess.

Most of our girls went into town to teachers' college or to nursing school. Boys who got to go to high school and normal school weren't coming back. Good farms came up for sale cheap. Up-and-coming farmers with progressive ideas were snapping up the neighbours' farms, buying their first tractors, four-furrow plows, eight-foot binders and more cattle. If you didn't expand, you had to sell out.

Gosh, before anyone started thinking about four-lane highways, this country was a funny mixture of good, bad and innocent. A farm would have maybe a dozen or 16 cows that didn't give much milk. They practically dried up in Winter. There was a barrel-chested bull with a brass ring in his nose and a frustrated glare in his eyes because there was always at least one of the cows in need of his attention. There were six brood sows in sties where the hard-packed manure built up through the Winter. When Spring came you bumped your head on the white-washed beams as you forked out the manure. The work horses seemed to walk right out of their shoes and we were always buying new collar pads for them in those long, sweaty days of haying and harvesting.

The mortgage didn't amount to much. The interest rate was low, three and a half, four percent. You could always borrow a couple of hundred from the bank to tide you over until the milk cheque came in. Nobody had much cash. The annual donation to the missionary and maintenance fund at the church was small. Christmas presents were always little and useful: a pound of tea that was supposed to last all year, an orange in the toe of the stocking, a $2 book of worthwhile literature. Oh, it was the mortgage and repairs to the ancient horse-drawn equipment that had to be paid first.

The kitchen was the heart of it all. Everybody – including the hired man if you could afford one – ate all their meals there. The flowered oil cloth was easy to wipe clean and protected the cherry table from food spills. At night, after chores, the family sat around the table and took turns with *The Farmer's Advocate*, *The Family Herald and Weekly Star* and *The London Free Press*. Bedtime was early.

Going to town Saturday night was as close to Sodom and

Gomorrah as a teenager would get. After a lukewarm bath, you smarmed your hair down with Brilliantine, put on your good wool pants, a white shirt and a wool sweater. The faithful old '29 Chevy was too small for everybody who wanted to go, but we packed ourselves in anyway. Town had an ice cream parlour, the movies (*Africa Speaks*, Harold Lloyd dangling from the minute hand of the city hall clock, fallen women smoking), hanging 'round the garage, watching the "Ladies with Escorts" entrance to the hotel, patrolling both sides of Main Street, trying to catch the attention of that Summer's heart's desire, trying not to be stupid.

Sunday was the day off. Church was mandatory. Funny thing, it was always a surprise to see all those boys we knew, up there singing bass and baritone in the choir. Their brown suits were a tad too short for them. Their shirt collars seemed half a size

The main street of Aylmer, Elgin County.

too small. Their foreheads were white, because their weekday straw hats kept the sun off.

Church was better than Saturday night in town because we could look for long minutes at our heart's desire in the pew ahead and wonder (no, agonize) if, when and how the great "physical" mysteries would ever be solved.

It was a world without margarine, carcinogens, triglycerides or cholesterol. There were no pesticides or weed killers to accumulate in the livers of birds and fish. Sclerosis was something the doctor knew very little about. Hearts were muscles that failed finally.

It was a world of fences that needed fixing all the time; a world of stubborn affection for "the good earth," a wholesome sense of possession that sometimes turned inside out and became a sense of being possessed and controlled by the farm that could barely produce enough to meet the mortgage payments.

The barn was filled each summer with tons of hay. There was practically no automation. The hay loader lifted it off the ground onto the wagon; but someone had to build the load with a hay fork so the wagon wouldn't tip over on the way to the barn. The slings or fork lifted the hay off the wagon into the mow; but someone had to get up into the mow and mow it away and salt it down by hand. At harvest time, the straw blower of the threshing machine was aimed into the end of the barn so there would be enough bedding straw for the cows, horses and pigs through the long Winter.

"Spontaneous combustion" was the first big mouthful of an idea that farm children learned. Hay that had not been dried properly could generate enough internal heat inside the barn to turn black and ignite.

Late in the Spring when they were empty, the high barns were targets for those shreds of high winds that shriek randomly out of Michigan across the flatlands. Communal barn raisings (like the threshing dinners) became the outward display of a powerful sense of community in the country – the community that is still seen as the sweet alternative to the loneliness of the urban crowd.

There is a museum quality to these nostalgic yearnings of city people.

They look back. Things lasted longer back then. Things didn't break down. Life was deliberate and even tempered. They look back and wish they could *go* back because old is best; yesterday was better. Today is unmanageable. What's new is unpredictable, accident prone, quick to betray.

City people are custodians of an uncertain world now. Governments that weren't supposed to topple, toppled. Big companies – big important companies that could never go bankrupt – went bankrupt. Packard. Nash. Studebaker. Chrysler. Massey Ferguson. White. International. Dome. Even banks are in trouble. In Canada? Go on, the government will never let a chartered bank go belly up. Oh no?

New viruses terrorize the population. Trainloads of chemicals

Loyalist graveyard,
Williamstown,
Glengarry County.

fall off the tracks. The biggest, safest jets fall out of the sky. Policemen die in the peaceable kingdom. Never knowing which solid pillar is going to crumble next, no longer able to see a day or two into the future, people look everywhere for some stability to shore them up in their uncertainties.

Bring back the good old days! Like it was back on the farm!

Today, the barns are long and low; too low for a high wind to decapitate. Haymows have been made obsolete by silos that are filled and emptied automatically. Straw for bedding has disappeared.

Today the southern Ontario landscape is a cluster of high silos every quarter of a mile, fat blue cathedrals of plenty that soar above a nineteenth-century homestead nearby, and the new split-level for Grandma and Grandpa next door.

The little churches that were once the social glue for all the families on two or three concessions are mostly empty now, or converted to apple storage, or a second home for someone from the city, or they are re-opened once a year for decoration day in the burial yard.

Today the men with white foreheads have expertise in raising pure bred animals, in animal nutrition and health, in the chemistry of soils, fertilizers, pesticides, herbicides, miticides, growth retardants, soil and water conservation.

Now farming is no longer an endurance contest. Today's generation of farmers has not experienced a depression. That has taken a lot of the old melancholy out of rural isolation. Farming is an intellectual challenge that involves big loans at the bank, big cash flows, inexplicable animal sickness, a growing season too wet or too dry, inexperienced part-time help at $4.50 an hour, depressed or unstable markets, flash floods in the Spring, windstorms in the Summer.

Doesn't anything ever stay the same?

3   *It's a Long Way to the End of the Row*

T HIS IS THE LIFE. They've got everything: blankets and chairs, cold drinks, junk food, real food and the best place on the beach. This is the only way to celebrate the end of Winter, the arrival of Spring.

Smelt by the millions will be shimmering towards the shoreline tonight, so all day the Ambassador Bridge has been a steady stream of vans and pick-ups full of smelt freaks en route to their favourite and secret netting places along the Canadian side of

Lake Erie. This morning at eight o'clock, mom, dad and the two kids went through Customs and Immigration, past Kilometre Zero, where the 401 begins in the suburbs south of Windsor, and angled down to Point Pelee. Dad wanted to be right on the tip of Pelee because he'd always had good luck there.

It's a long hike from the parking lot to the far end of the Point, especially when you're lugging two Coleman gas lamps whose light will lure the fish to the beach, a box about the size of a small coffin full of ice to put the fish in, four deck chairs, a case of Pepsi, a case of beer, the dog, blankets, frisbees, magazines, food and the smelt net rolled on two long sticks.

They were first into the parking lot and first onto the beach. The kids like the freedom. Mom likes the warming sun and closes her eyes and listens to dad as he jams the Pepsi and beer bottles into the gravel in the shallow water to keep cool. Then he lays the twelve feet of gill net out along the beach. There is nothing to do now but wait for darkness and the silvery green fish vibrating just below the surface of the water.

As effortlessly as the weather, other American fishermen, cottagers and daytrippers flow across the Ambassador Bridge, like this Chrysler worker and his family. They pause briefly at Canadian Customs and Immigration, then drive into the flatlands of Essex County where food is cheap, camping spaces are clean and generous, traffic is light and the countryside is close.

Now this weather that breezes across the Ambassador Bridge so casually, not stopping for Customs inspection, is not just your idle chit-chat kind of weather. You can hear fear and frustration in the voices of the farmers in southwestern Ontario when they talk about it. Here is a countryside blessed with rich soil and the longest growing season in eastern Canada – yet it's hammered by wind out of control and water out of control like nowhere else in the country.

Weather sweeps into Essex County across the land bridge where the narrow Detroit River separates Canada from the U.S.A. Great convections of air build up in Nebraska and begin their voyage from West to East. If fragments of the warm air masses break off and become tornados, the only way they can enter Canada is across land. A tornado loses its energy over open water. It can keep up its destructive force only for a few hundred yards over Lake Erie or Lake St. Clair; but it can spin across the narrow Detroit and raise hell with crops and barns deep in Essex, Lambton, Kent and Middlesex Counties because there's nothing to stop it. There have been 19 destructive tornados in recent years. Three of them were multi-million-dollar disasters. A tornado can hit every 15 months in this area. At any other given point on

Great convections of air sweep across Essex County.

the map, there could be a tornado once in every 2,000 years.

The probability of a natural calamity is high. Farmers can expect 30 hours of freezing rain every year and they know they'll get one severe freezing-rain storm every five years.

Between May and September, 30 thunderstorms annually rumble across the rich flatlands – generally between noon and five o'clock. There are no lakes to dissipate them, no hills to divert them. One damaging hailstorm occurs once a year. A severe hailstorm hits every other year and a "beaut" will destroy millions of dollars worth of crops every seven years. Fifteen hailstorms were recorded in one 10-year period; 17 in another 19-year period.

A 100-year study of its antics shows that the Thames river is going to flood dangerously every four and a half years, causing some crop damage. The Thames drains parts of five counties and seems to prefer rampaging during the month of March.

The conscientious pessimist also knows there will be a serious drought every 50 years in this part of the country.

Field crops, fruit trees, vegetable crops start to peak between May and September. Strong winds and hail do their worst damage to them then because they are in mid-growth and can't recover. Not enough growing time is left for the farmer to re-seed where the crops have been beaten down.

Mother Nature can be an ill-tempered old bitch in Essex County. Who wants to put up with it?

It is an orange science-fiction turtle – more robot than animal – creeping slowly along the row of tomato plants, its indiscriminate snout snuffling up red tomatoes, green tomatoes, vines, clumps of dirt. Under the white canvas carapace, six people cling like barnacles to the sides of the creature. They stare at the tomatoes tumbling along the conveyor belt to the elevator that plucks the red ones and places them into the 12-ton box trailer crawling alongside. The people wear surgical masks. A hand darts forward suddenly and snatches a green tomato or a clump of wet soil. On both sides of the beast's humming stomach a green glow shines on the tomatoes and reflects up on the faces of the people. Behind, the beast expels the green tomatoes, the vines and the dirt that have been rejected by the green electronic glow. In an hour and a half the beast has ingested more than 25 tons of red tomatoes and spewed them into the trailers.

The turtle is a $130,000 Blackwelder tomato harvester. It first snuffled into California, where it allowed farmers to reduce the number of migrant pickers from 40,000 to 8,000. It also increased their output by three times. Self-propelled, it straddles the row of tomato vines, cuts them below ground level and lifts everything up into the high-speed rollers that separate the tomatoes from the vines. The tomatoes – red, orange, green and white – tumble through the electronic colour sorter. Only the red and orange ones are allowed to go through. There is an electronic sorter on both sides of the harvester. Each sorter costs $27,000.

There are tomato harvesters without the electronic sorters. They cost less, but they need twelve people riding along to do the colour sorting manually.

Agriculture is a $200 million industry in Essex County. The largest single crop is tomatoes – $50 million worth of early greenhouse and field tomatoes last year. Field tomatoes are grown principally for ketchup and tomato paste.

Terrence Wright, Harrow, Ontario, is the owner of the Blackwelder. For Terry, the tomato year begins when he signs a contract with the Heinz company in Leamington to deliver a certain number of tons of tomatoes at a price that is agreed on before the tomatoes are planted.

"Then it's up to us to bring them in with something left over for us."

The price is negotiated by the Vegetable Growers' Marketing Board, with the Processors' Association. The processors appear to have an advantage in this negotiation. They can bring tomato paste in from countries where labour costs are lower than Canada's. "If you don't like the price we can bring in more paste from Bulgaria."

That's the pressure that makes the tomato grower hunt for corners to cut, that makes the Blackwelder harvester an attractive alternative to hand sorting, provided there are at least 100 acres in tomatoes to justify its cost. The grower is forced to think as big as the processor.

On average the grower gets six cents a pound for the thick-skinned tomato. He must plan on harvesting at least 20 tons of tomatoes from each acre of land. If there is no mortgage on the farm, if the interest rate on his operating loan at the bank is low, if he has paid for his tractors, harvester, trailers and other machinery and they are in good repair, if his family provides some low-cost or no-cost labour, then the grower might be able to pay himself 3/10ths of a cent on the six cents a pound he receives.

It's a long way to the end of the row.

The Essex County farmer's small talk is about big money. It is not a matter of greed. It is a question of survival. His income depends on three things: the contract price negotiated for him by his marketing board, his ability to keep costs under control and the weather, the weather, the weather.

If he has 100 acres in tomatoes, he can expect a harvest of 2,000 tons at $115 a ton for a gross income of $230,000, when he delivers the tomatoes to the processor in August and September. That sounds like a big income until you track down all the costs.

The grower pays $21,900 for 115,500 baby plants in the Spring.

He pays $10,000 for four different kinds of fertilizers.

He pays $14,000 for herbicides, fungicides, insecticides and ripeners.

He pays $14,700 for hired hands to plant, hoe, sort and drive.

He pays $5,000 for crop insurance.

He pays $3,400 for marketing and grading fees.

He pays $11,600 for repairs and service on tractors, the harvester and other machinery.

He pays $1,900 interest on his six-month operating loan at the bank.

He pays $1,500 for expenses like the phone, electricity, accounting, soil tests.

If he keeps a professional set of books, as all big farmers do, some fixed costs will be charged against the gross income.

Semi-skilled labour will get $5,400.

He will pay himself $11,000 as a management allowance.

There will be $54,500 in depreciation, interest, insurance and storage of the tractors, the harvester, the other machinery and trucks.

A land charge of $25,000 will be some combination of interest and principal on a mortgage.

Total costs: $189,500.

That would result in a return of $40,500 if everything fell into place. But things don't fall into place quite so neatly.

Costs are always too close to gross income for comfort. Bad weather can mean more man-hours to do the harvesting. Too much rain at the wrong time of year could mean extra expense, because two tractors are needed to haul the tomatoes through some low spots in the field. Hail is always a risk. Sorters you were counting on decide not to work this year and you have to pay more than you budgeted. The harvester decides to be cantankerous and it can't be repaired under the service contract. Bank rates jump.

Lunch at the Wrights' today is a dieter's dream: cabbage salad, beans, tomatoes, cantaloupe, raspberries, blueberries and milk. Young Greg has a ham sandwich because he eats to a different drummer.

The radio is tuned to the CBC station in Windsor. One television set is tuned to a Detroit station. The other is tuned to Toledo. Terry sits at the head of the table where he can keep an eye on the two TV weather reports. "Most of our weather comes across the lake from Ohio. Toledo is generally pretty accurate. The Detroit forecast is better than the CBC because the CBC is forecasting more for the pilots at the Windsor airport." Conversation stops abruptly when the Toledo radar scanner comes on.

The daily communion with the high priests of low pressure systems takes about ten minutes. Terry gives his full attention to lunch, but there is a detached look on his face. The weather forecast for the rest of the day and tomorrow determine when he will call for a tractor to make up a train of trailers and go to Leamington. Four full ones sit in the yard now, one of them holds 25 tons. He must remember to tell the sorters he will want them tomorrow and probably Saturday if the rain holds off.

How much faith do you put in the self-assured weatherman who dazzles you with satellite maps and sinuous weather fronts and forecasts? They withhold the facts a grower needs. Don't tell us what it's going to do in Essex County tomorrow morning. Tell us what it's going to do in the 20 acres of tomatoes just west of the new orchard.

"Someday I'll have a monitor here and be able to plug into

a weather radar system that will show the local rainstorms moving across all the farms between Amherstberg and here."

Kevin, 12, and Rodney, 10, are serious Detroit Tigers fans. There is not much to be fanatical about this year. Everybody is beating the World's Champions. Mathematically there may be a chance for them to roll back into first place but the Blue Jays and the Yankees would really have to fall apart in September.

"How about those Blue Jays?" Terry asks; but by now it is just half-hearted, well-worn teasing that doesn't get a rise out of the boys. Besides, the Jays have frittered away an eight-game lead and the Yankees are only one and a half games behind and there's all of September still to play.

Terry and Joy Wright and their three children are the second and third generations of Wrights to grow fruits and vegetables

The Wright brothers are home from school.

here. Terry's parents run a drive-in fruit and vegetable stand just down the road across from the golf course. Together the Wrights farm more than 300 acres.

Terry Wright is like farmers from one end of the 401 to the other. He likes what he's doing. He likes what he's accomplished. He enjoys most of the strategy and tactics of fighting for a profit in the cost-price squeeze. Still, he carries around inside him the "what if" that shocks and excites him at the same time.

"What if I sold out, paid off whatever debt there is left and invested the remainder? Would I make more in interest and dividend income than I do now?"

There is no wind. There is no sun. The precise rows of onions find infinity in the blue haze half a mile away. Black dust from the black muck soil covers the pick-up truck, the onion harvester, the Romanian tractor, the dark forearms and troubled face of Walter Cherneski. His mind is churning with the tiresome arithmetic of breaking even on his 100 acres of onions. Every time he goes over the figures, the results have an ominous feel. Armstrong's are paying $3 for a 50-pound bag this year. That works out to six cents a pound. That's just about the same price the tomato growers get.

Walter relights his pipe and glances around. The diked landscape is flat. The landmarks are small, subtle and far away. Lake Erie is invisible behind the dike. He can see the tops of the cottages. Far to the north somebody is loading a tractor trailer

Harvesting onions, Essex County.

with carrots. In the west an onion harvester is struggling through a field that has as many weeds as it has onions. The grower was late with the herbicide spray.

The Summer has not been typical. Walter's 90-day onions are still ripening 120 days after he planted them and the 120-day onions are ready to harvest now, just 90 days after planting. The mystical combination of sun and drying winds didn't happen the way it usually does. The season got off to a bad start. Last April Walter planted a 20-acre patch of Spartan Sleepers. The next day a stiff north-east wind swept down the long curve of Point Pelee and took the freshly planted seed with it. He had to replant.

The weather forecasts are not promising. If there was any hope of some drying wind or a few days of cloudless sun, it would be best to wait for them, but the Toledo forecast is for more of the same: overcast, light winds, high humidity.

Walter climbs into the seat of the Romanian "Universal" tractor which is pulling the long onion harvester and four box trailers. He sets the power take-off that drives the harvester, puts the tractor into its slowest gear. The wheels straddle the row. At this speed, the row seems to have no end. The drone of the tractor, the steady clatter of the harvester isolate the grower from the rest of the world. He is encased in a cocoon of sound where he watches the jaws of the harvester as it swallows up the row of onions. He glances back at the elevator that takes the onions from the harvester and drops them into the box trailer far behind. He makes minuscule adjustments to the hydraulic

Harvesting onions, Essex County.

system that raises and lowers the jaws of the harvester. He rarely touches the steering wheel because ruts between the rows of onions keep the tractor on course. The end of the row is a long way away. He has time to think. He has time to explore the classic pessimism of the farmer. He has time to worry. If his neighbour sold 25 tons of onions to wholesalers in Bradford, north of Toronto, does that mean the local market is plugged up? This fall he has to renegotiate the lease for the 46 acres south of D sideroad. He can't afford an increase in the rent if onions stay at $3 a bag. If interest rates keep going down, will he be able to renegotiate the 12% mortgage at the Royal Bank? He feeds his pessimism with the bitter recollection of the T-D telling him to "have $200,000 here in 10 days, Walter." He hopes to spray some growth inhibitor on a field near home before dark. He looks ahead. The end of the row is a long way away.

Walter Cherneski's odyssey to the Pelee marshlands began in Manitoba. His mother and father were young Polish immigrants who were allotted 160 acres of prairie, on condition that a crude house and barn would be built within two years. Walter began early to help his father in the short growing season of the West and in the harsh cold of the long winters.

"I remember I had to stand on a box to put the harness on the team of horses."

One cold January, his father went to a town 40 miles away to buy a second team of horses and he rode the team home through the penetrating cold. A month later, his father was dead of pneumonia. His mother died a few months later and the Cherneski children scattered like seeds in the wind.

Walter went to Winnipeg and heard that Red Lake Gold Mines were taking on men. He signed on, went to Red Lake and found he liked the underground work. He was mucking ore and being paid by the ton. He was making $18 a day. In Red Lake an expensive hobby caught his fancy: cards. There were weeks when he would lose most of his pay.

He took his newfound addiction to Toronto, where he got a job in a munitions factory in New Toronto punching out discs for artillery shells. At the end of the war, Walter got a job at the Florentine Lamp Company. He was making $18 for a 44-hour week.

Then he met Olga.

It was at a Ukrainian–Orthodox wedding. Walter – in a shiny rented tuxedo – was an usher. The groom was one of his best buddies. Relatives of the bride came up to Toronto from Leamington for the wedding.

Walter was introduced to Olga and that was pretty well it. Within a few weeks Walter and Olga became "an item." She persuaded Walter to return to Leamington with her and try to make a go of it there.

"I gave up the cards. I never was a drinker so I didn't have to give that up."

Forty years later all the weather forecasts are wrong. There isn't a cloud in the morning sky. The benevolent sun massages the endless rows of onions. A dry north-west wind riffles through the onion tops. Sixteen box trailers full of onions are lined up outside the Cherneski warehouse waiting to be sorted and packed. Olga – eyes flashing with suspicion – is poised at the front end of the sorting machine. The elevator rumbles into action. Olga's hands flash into the onions and cull bits of muck, weeds and tops that got through the harvester. The onions tumble along the belt. The first-grade ones go to the end of the sorting machine, where they make a sharp right turn and plop into the red fishnet bags.

Two of the Cherneski boys lift the bags to the weigh scales, top them up until each weighs 50 pounds, tie them and stack them in sixty-bag cubes. The fork lift truck whisks them away to wait for the truck from Armstrong's.

Down on the Marenpettit marsh, Walter has groomed half a dozen rows of onions with a machine that simply lifts and tumbles the plants and leaves them sitting on top of the black muck, ready for the harvester. An acre of this light, organic soil on top

Canal by Marenpettit Marsh, Essex County.

Olga and Walter Cherneski, Mersea Township.

of clay is worth $9,250. You can rent an acre for a year for $700. Spartan Sleepers, Cromney Downings, Rockets, Taurus, Canada Maple – these are the varieties of storage onions that burgeon into the cash flow of Cherneski & Sons, Onions, Leamington, Ontario.

The unexpected sun and breeze seduce Walter, but not completely. He stops the tractor and climbs down, favouring the

right knee that got bruised the other day when he slipped in the mud. He re-lights his pipe. A million seagulls squat on the black soil. Behind him on the dike is a Van Gogh blaze of sunflowers. He identifies every pick-up truck that drives by.

The litany of the cost-price squeeze goes on. "I get six cents a pound. They sell for 69 cents in the supermarket. We need floor prices. Somebody should be monitoring supermarket prices. Mortgage assistance is a good idea for farmers. I don't know what the answer is. I've got a 12% mortgage. I've got an operating line of credit up to $90,000. I've got a line of credit up to $40,000 for equipment maintenance. We have to spray for midges, thrips, bugs and weeds. We have to take our chances every year on whatever the price is at harvest time."

Surely there is a bright side to it all on this bright August morning.

"I eat raw onions two or three times a week. In a sandwich. It's good for the blood."

Anything else?

"I don't have to punch a goddamned time clock."

The road and canal beside Marenpettit Marsh, Essex County.

He squints across the great black flat of the marshland and a tractor pulling six empty box trailers emerges from behind the row of poplars where side road D crosses the road on top of the dike. It is his grandson. It means the people in the warehouse have sorted all but a few of the onions and will need more to keep the sorting and bagging machines busy. He tamps a fresh wad of tobacco into his pipe. It's time to start down the long, slow row again.

4   *The Seedlings of Change*

FALL BROUGHT TO THE ELGIE FARM the old familiar reminder that there was a lot needed doing before freeze-up.

Now the days are shorter than the nights. No one knows when the first frost will come. Most of the leaves have dropped from the soy-bean plants. There are three acres of tomatoes still to be picked, winter wheat to be planted, corn and beans to be harvested, the silo to be filled, one more cut of hay.

This time of year Kent is a sea of tasselled corn waiting to be

Umber stems and pods of soybeans in rows of Oriental austerity.

cut – corn that grows in regimented rows close to the edges of the concession roads. Only the roofs of the barns and houses are visible from the road over the top of the corn. The cobs are heavy. The stalks and leaves are tan and autumn. The red-tailed hawks ride the thermals and swoop with sudden ferocity behind the corn.

Where there is no corn, there are soy beans. They are a nondescript tangled mass of leaves turning yellow until they drop off and reveal umber stems and pods in rows and rows of Oriental austerity. This year the price is austere too.

Earl is working on the oil pressure gauge of the White diesel tractor. There's a new implement attached to the White – a heavy welded frame with long solid steel teeth spaced across it. It will lift old rows of branches and bushes up to free them from the weeds and soil and pile them for burning. It was designed and built by one of the neighbours.

Bill is, somehow, wrapped around the underside of the three-furrow plow taking off a seized-up disc coulter. His dad, Ken Elgie, hands him the socket wrench and he taps with the ball-pean hammer when Bill says to. As soon as they clean and free

Earl and Bill Elgie reassemble combine's main bearing.

up the bearing on the coulter, Ken will plough the early corn stubble until it is too dark to see.

Earl and Bill are the fifth generation of Elgies to farm this land in Kent County. The first of the Elgies in Canada was George, who came over from Scotland in the 1860s and bought 100 acres from the Taylor family. (The Taylor descendants now run the grain elevators over at Tupperville.) George must have been a good farmer because he helped set up farms for each of his five sons. Today, Ken, the fourth generation, is in an affectionate, rewarding business partnership with Earl and Bill.

This year the Elgies had a contract to grow 30 acres of to-matoes for Hunt's in Tilbury; a contract to grow popping corn for an outfit in Blenheim (Ken smiles the half-smile, half-wince of the conscientious risk-taker when he recalls an earlier con-tract for popping corn that paid off at 10 cents to the dollar after the processor went bankrupt); a contract for butternut squash with Olmsteads in Wheatley (Labatt's just bought them out); contracts to grow seed corn and seed soy beans for Pioneer in Ridgetown. On top of that, they grew winter wheat and com-mercial corn and sold it to local grain dealers. They keep a herd of 21 Hereford cows and a Hereford bull. They fatten all the calves to full market weight and sell them through the auction-eer at Talbotville.

It was not always this way. The Elgies grew burley tobacco until their quota got so small it wasn't worth the effort. They

Earl Elgie serves nephew, William, at lunch.

grew sweet corn, peppers and white beans. ("When we were kids that's all we did: hoe white beans," Earl remembers.) They kept chickens and sold the eggs. They had pigs and dairy cattle. They sold cream to the dairy and fed the skimmed milk to the pigs.

Earl Elgie, B.Sc.(Ag), graduated from the University of Guelph in 1978. Bill Elgie got his diploma from the Ridgetown College of Agricultural Technology in 1979. So it was that the nature of

Earl Elgie watches bumper crop of corn fill trailer bin.

the conversations between father and sons began to change in the Summer of '79. The boys had picked up new ideas about fertilizer, cattle feed and ventilation for the barns.

The Elgies are of two minds about economies of scale. They think more about cutting operating costs and squeezing more revenue out of each acre than they do about expanding their 700 acres of owned or leased land. Bill used the beginning farmers' assistance plan to buy 70 acres of sandy brushland near Thamesville. He had a drainage system put in, at a cost of probably $600 an acre. Earl bought 50 acres of "scruffy clay" up in Lambton County.

It is doubtful their little herd of Herefords will grow much larger. A couple of dozen animals with a resident bull don't make strenuous daily demands on their time. They keep the herd because "we've always had Herefords"; but in the next few years they will likely shift from Herefords to cross-breeds of Charolais or Limousin with Herefords.

"The cross-breeds seem to get a few extra pennies a pound at the auctions."

When the time comes to make the decision for or against cross-breeds, everybody in the Elgie clan will be involved. Change does not happen overnight in the life of a farmer. Management issues are discussed during "supper at Mom's" once a week. "Mom's" is the home of Kenneth and Ruth Elgie – the two-story Victorian cottage that used to be the parsonage of the Methodist Church of Dawn Mills. The church closed its doors in 1967. When Ken and Ruth moved in, this made the hired man's cottage available for Bill and Loree. Earl and Nancy live in the old Elgie homestead.

This Wednesday night, "dinner at Mom's" has been changed to "dinner at Loree's." Ruth brings a creamy cabbage salad in a big crystal bowl. Loree serves her slithery, tomato-y lasagna whose melted cheese slings like fine telephone lines from your mouth to the fork. Earl and Bill picked a bushel of sweet corn at the leased farm up the road. Nancy brought the hot rolls. A dark-chocolate cake with mocha icing and chocolate ice cream on the side appears with the coffee.

There are no real issues to discuss tonight. Instead there is the acknowledgement of the change that touches them all with the arrival of Fall. Nancy is back at her job as a teacher's aide at a school where mentally retarded children are taught beside the other kids. Earl remembers how much he hated the yellow bus that took him the two miles into Dresden. Bill remembers how grateful he was that he could drive with his mother, who taught in Dresden.

It is a night of light nostalgia. Ruth remembers the school years of their four daughters and two sons. She always thought her children were shy while they were growing up. Ken remembers when Earl got his driver's licence in the '67 Plymouth. That was the year the church closed and the year they all piled into the tiny camper trailer to go to Expo. Bill remembers courting Loree with the '71 Fargo pick-up. Loree remembers wishing he

Ruth Elgie, Dawn Mills, Kent County.

could have arrived in something else. Ken remembers further back, when 120 gallons of gas were all he needed for a year in the pick-up and the car. He shakes his head in amazement. "A hundred and twenty gallons. Imagine that. I remember there were ads in the Detroit papers in those days. Five gallons for a dollar."

Bill totes up the work left to do before freeze-up. Suddenly it is nearly midnight, time for sleep. The night sky is clear. The moon and the stars are definite. There will be no frost.

Next morning, long after Loree and Nancy had gone to work, Ken was in third gear with the plow set shallow in the sandy loam, and Bill and Earl were getting ready to test the new brush-pushing implement. Then Ruth came out of the parsonage. She told Earl that the schedule clerk at Hunt's had phoned. Hunt's wanted ten tons of tomatoes by one o'clock Friday.

At that moment the Mennonite family who had come to the

Ken Elgie and the reluctant bolt.

Elgies' from northwestern Ontario, for the tomato harvest, stepped out of their mobile home and climbed into their car. The mother and father and teenaged children were showered and shiny in their going-to-town clothes. They and the Elgies had agreed to this day off. They were on their way to Aylmer to visit with Mennonite friends and to shop for clothing before returning to Lake of the Woods.

Ruth, Bill and Earl looked at each other. They said nothing as the car went out the lane. They were not going to change the plans of the Mennonite family at the very last minute. The Mennonites had been good, conscientious pickers. The season was nearly over. They did some fast mental arithmetic and decided they could pick the 10 tons of tomatoes themselves between ten o'clock Thursday and noon Friday. Ruth would pick, although she normally didn't.

Ruth, bandanna'd and youthful, set to work in one row, Bill in another, Earl in another. Bent or kneeling, they work their way down the long rows as the sun works its way across the sky. It is ideal weather. Old Fred, the arthritic Irish setter, and Duke, the sociable black Lab, sun themselves in the soy-bean field next to the tomatoes. From time to time they come and mooch a ripe tomato from Bill or Earl.

The tomatoes are a small thick-skinned variety that came to the Elgie farm last Spring in a small box from Georgia. The box contained 50,000 seedlings, each about six inches tall. There was

Bill Elgie plugs in the auger.

no soil to protect the roots or to separate one plant from another. Each plant had to be separated delicately by hand and put into the planting machine.

The hours pass. Soon it will be dinner time. Ruth gets up and paces the length of the row she has picked. She counts baskets full of tomatoes and comes back to where Bill and Earl are still picking.

"Well, look, if I picked 56 baskets you boys surely picked 70 each."

Bill and Earl look at each other and laugh. They would have 10 tons ready by noon tomorrow.

"That's right, Maw. You just keep on building up our egos."

5   *Katie Kauffman's Dynasty of Hope*

THERE IS NO TELEPHONE in this Amish house. There is no electricity. Light comes from kerosene lamps. The ironing is done with a pressurized gas iron.

"We don't live out of the supermarkets," John says. "Everything we eat comes from the garden, from the farm. We can our vegetables and meat and keep them cool down the cellar. We've already started eating early onions. They're my favourite."

Their voices – sometimes in English, sometimes in German – disappear in the rising, rain-filled wind. John and his wife Katie agree with each other before they do anything on the farm: where to scuffle, where to pull the cord taut to mark another row, which beans to plant, how far apart, how deep. They have done this many times before. It is a peaceable ritual of consultation because they both know what needs doing. It was foreordained by generations of Amish self-reliance. It has been taught to them by their mothers and fathers, grandmothers and grandfathers.

Absalom – Katie's father-in-law – comes out of the grandfather house and walks a few slow paces to the door leading to the back shed. He carries a cane, but uses it lightly. There is the inscrutable smile of the ancient on his translucent face. Tenderly, his son, John, reaches over to straighten the old man's collar.

"Where are you going?"

"To get a few sticks of wood."

"No, no, let me get them for you."

"Don't fuss. I'm getting them." Absalom disappears into the gloom of the shed. His wife died six weeks ago. He is alone and lonely now. Cataracts obstruct his vision badly; but he is self-reliant. He gets his own breakfast and supper in the grandfather house. He eats with John and Katie and their boys at the noon meal. He tends his fire. He knows the daily rhythms of the farm – his farm – and, although he can't see that far, he knows which fields the three boys are working in and what they are doing as the planting season comes to an end.

"We look after each other," says John. "It is our way. The only time an old person leaves the family is if he gets to be a danger to himself."

"We don't believe in insurance of any kind. Insurance would prevent us from doing our duty to look after each other. We can't let outside organizations take that away from us. It is the way we were brought up. It is what we believe. We have good doctors in Ingersoll. Katie was over there the other day with pains in her ribs. She'll have to go back. They're good doctors. We pay cash. People outside have O.H.I.P. We don't because it is our duty to be self-reliant. Yes, we pay municipal taxes and we pay the federal taxes."

Katie is planting beans in the vegetable garden. She is wearing her usual long brown dress over rubber boots. She paces the lengths of the rows quickly, deftly breaking up lumps with the hoe. There is an intense, concentrated look on her face. A few drops of rain fall.

John Kauffman helps Katie get the seeds in before the heavy, steady rain that has been promised for later in the day. He picks up a hand scuffler and works up the soil under the binder twine stretched taut between two sticks. The scuffler is like a fine-toothed rototiller with no motor. He pushes and pulls it down the unseeded row and leaves lusty, fine-textured dirt for the seed beans. Katie doles out the beans, then covers them and tamps the dirt down with the hoe.

Their children, Levi, John and Joni – 17, 15 and 12 – did all the work of Spring planting this year: grooming the rolling fields that had been ploughed last Fall, sowing the corn, oats and barley and packing the soil down after with the pulverizer. It is the last time Joni will need Levi's help to harness the horses because Joni is growing like a weed.

A dark and luminous cloud hangs out to the west. The eastern sky has the bright look of a storm about to happen. The wind is uncertain in the big shade trees along the road. It is going to rain. Katie's timing is just right. The new seeds will get a proper soaking this afternoon.

Old clay drainage tiles, rusty, de-bottomed oil cans and vinegar jugs protect the fragile new tomato and celery plants from the wind, sun, frost and birds. In a few days it will be time to plant the potatoes. The freshly cultivated land is ready for them.

The Kauffman farmyard is a portrait of tradition and stability. The L-shaped strawberry patch is vibrating with masses of white, star-shaped blooms – each the promise of a fat, red berry a few weeks from now. Ancient clumps of blue iris grow in the fence line around the garden. Across the lane in the field south of the barn, the just-milked Holsteins ruminate. Fritz, the farm dog, with his tail in a stiff curl, makes a leisurely patrol of the yard. He pays no attention to the rooster and bantam hens that strut under the wheels of the black buggy. From this distance, in this wind, you can barely hear the Leghorns bragging about that morning's production in the hen house.

Whenever a car or truck passes, John and Katie glance over to see if they know the driver. Usually there is a quick wave of recognition without missing a stroke of the hoe or scuffler. It is the kind of gesture that says, "Ah, there you are, out there, and here we are in here. It's good to acknowledge our humanity in this silence and in this separation."

Katie moves quickly now, because she has promised to go and work with one of her daughters-in-law today. She knows exactly how long it takes to cover the six miles with the horse and buggy. She will not be late.

Levi, driving a team of matched Belgians, heads out the lane with a wagonload of old creamery cans. The cans will be filled with gas for his older brother's stationary engine. Young John

Six miles by horse and buggy.

gets the horse and buggy ready for his mother's trip. Joni is in the house getting cleaned up for school. Wet, black curls halo his wide, handsome face under the straw hat.

Fritz the farm dog looks for a comfortable place before the rain comes. He is only faintly interested in strangers who talk to his master. He flops down on the side porch and watches John go from building to building in the farmyard.

In the barn, there is a pen with eight baby Holstein bull calves. The Kauffmans buy them when they are a week old, from Oxford and Middlesex County dairy farmers who want to get rid of them right after birth, because their business is milk. Each one costs about $100. On the Kauffman farm the calves are fed until they reach 500 pounds. Then they are sold as veal calves for about 81 cents a pound. That sounds like $305 gross income per calf; but it takes nearly a year of care and feeding, so the net profit is small. Another pen in the barn has the four replacement heifers – young Holsteins that will be bred at the appropriate time to take the place of venerable cows in the milking herd. All but one of the 16 horse stalls are empty. Spring planting is done; there is no need of the horses today; they are out to pasture, except for the one that will take Katie to her oldest son Henry's farm today.

In the pig barn and on the side hill north of the house there are 24 sows in various stages of pregnancy. It is three months, three weeks and three days between conception and delivery of a sow's litter.

"There are some who say it is three months, three weeks, three days, three hours and three minutes," John says mildly.

The chicken house is crowded with white hens squawking the familiar Leghorn concerto. Eggs are collected every day and kept cool in five-dozen trays. Neighbours have standing orders for eggs from the Kauffmans. The boys take fresh eggs to sell at a farmers' market east of London.

Last year they had a bumper crop of Kennebec potatoes. They ran an ad in the local paper and sold a thousand bags.

There are five black buggies in the drive shed. One is a "democrat" – a long four-wheeler with two seat benches. It carries four comfortably but there are occasions when four adults and four children crowd in. Each buggy has a fluorescent triangle of red on the back.

The little white pump-house sits over a 60-foot drilled well. When Absalom Kauffman brought his family here 19 years ago there was an unreliable windmill standing where the pumphouse is now. The Kauffmans have modified a little lawn-mower engine to pump their water.

Pumping water, filling the silo and grinding grain are the only chores done by gas engines. Everything else is horse power and hand power. Firmly rooted convictions that are centuries old put them out of step with twentieth-century agribusiness. The plow, the cultivator, the stiff-tooth harrow, the disc, the pulverizer, the seed drill, the seven-foot Massey Harris grain binder, the rake, the mower, the hay wagon with the hat-loader behind the side-delivery rake – all of these are pulled by teams of toffee-coloured Belgians with bleached blonde manes and tails.

Thoughtless outsiders look in at the Amish world and misinterpret their industrious independence. Some say they are harmless, religious eccentrics. Others claim, with lightly concealed resentment, that they are anti-social and hostile to the progress that has been speeding past them now for about a hundred years.

What they are is a slow-paced minority of survivors. Four centuries ago their forefathers survived burnings at the stake, stonings, crucifixions, live burials, suffocations, whippings, the severing of tongues, hands, feet and ears. Their literary root – other than the Bible – is a book titled *The Bloody Theatre*, or *Martyrs' Mirror*. It was first published 350 years ago and is a gruelling encyclopaedia of eyewitness descriptions of savagery committed in the name of Christianity. It is the Amish man's metaphor for the eternal battle between the carnal and spiritual worlds. The battle is still being waged. The Amish strategy is to survive in small, spiritually homogeneous, self-sufficient com-

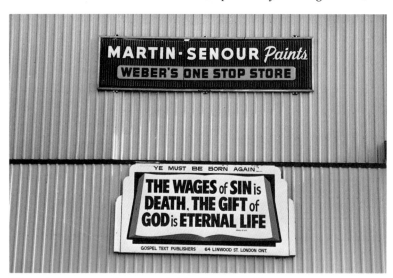

Waterloo county has a graphic flavour of its own.

Sometimes the message is not clear.

munities; to live with a simplicity and mutuality that emerge from their personal vision of what the New Testament means.

They do not sit in judgement of "the outside." They are too busy concentrating on living the life that qualifies them for salvation when their time comes.

The Amish man has been taught that it is the highest of family duties to prepare his young for the close-knit religious experience of his forefathers. To do this well, there is no need for education beyond grade eight – the age when it is legal to take a child out of the "outside" education system. The education that matters to the Amish is the wisdom of grandfather Absalom and father John and Mother Katie and older brother Henry. That's the education that matters, because "old is best."

Today's Amish trace their spiritual lineage back directly to a small group of Anabaptists, led out of the larger group of Swiss Brethren in the 1690s by Jakob Ammann, in Berne, Switzerland. Ammann and his followers broke away because they couldn't conform to the practices that had been established by the Brethren ever since 1525, when the Lutheran ferment was at its height in Europe.

Ammann's own practice of Christianity was quiet, passive. As the generations rolled by, the Amish never developed a rationale for self-defence and refused to defend their possessions. They saw themselves as "defenceless Christians." When they were in any kind of disagreement with the world outside, they would move to a new location rather than choose confrontation. From Switzerland they went to Germany, Holland, Russia and North America.

In their daily life in Canada they are frozen in time and pace somewhere at the end of the nineteenth century. They are a tiny group of people who, in their plain clothes and humble behaviour, choose to live in fixed, familiar tradition while the world outside lunges on to an unknown destination.

Their religion is a total way of life. In practice it involves fasting, informal mutual aid, keeping the young on the farm, limiting education, and sometimes "shunning" – voting unbelievers out of their community. They do not try to deny the larger world. Nor do they ever try to recruit outsiders into their church. They see themselves as "strangers and pilgrims" in today's society. The Amish man feels contact with the world through the labour of his muscles and the aching in his bones after the work is done. Work is proper and good.

They live in "a living hope of salvation"; so the idea that their salvation is certain is taboo.

"If I said 'I know I am saved' that would be boasting and vanity," John Kauffman says. "We can only hope."

The little Amish community of which the Kauffmans are part is different from other church sects because the rules governing the way they live are the traditional ways handed down from generation to generation by word of mouth. Nothing is written.

Married men in an Amish church district select their minister and deacon from their own ranks. The ministers select the bishop the same way. When a critical decision must be made there has to be unanimous consent of all adults baptized into the community. Critical? Suppose someone is to be expelled from the community. Suppose someone is to be received back into the community.

The married women contribute to the unanimous decision. The married women contribute more than unanimity. Division of labour may be by gender, but there is an overt, unforced consulting, helping, discussing between man and wife in all of the affairs of the day. The Amish family is not led by a bearded old tyrant in a straw hat.

The "churchness" of Amish people is in the Biblical sense of the word "church" – a joining of families who believe the same things about God and who agree on the route to salvation without help from specially educated and paid spiritual advisors. The Amish are a church without buildings.

Tradition puts limits on the size of an Amish church district. It is as big as the number of people who can pray and chant comfortably in an average-sized country home. It is as big as

Patient horse waits for its Amish driver.

the area horse-drawn buggies can cover every other Sunday, taking the plain people to the home of the family whose turn it is to provide the meeting place.

An Amish Sunday service begins at 9 o'clock. A bishop and a minister speak. They sing hymns and chant. There are deep silences between hymns. The service lasts three hours, then a noon dinner is served and it is time for conversation, keeping in touch. Most families are home before three o'clock.

The Kauffman house is plain and spacious with bare hardwood floors. There is an oil stove and a wood stove in the big kitchen, with two plain breakfronts, a table and chairs and shelves for the oil lamps. There is a small water room with a hand pump beside the kitchen.

In the big front room there is a space heater and a cradle and the ironing board is set up with the gas-powered iron on top. Chairs, some from Iowa, some from Canada, line the walls of

Amish school children near Aylmer.

the room. There are no pictures on the walls. There are two calendars.

"We like visiting zoos," John says. "We've been to the Toronto Zoo and the Detroit Zoo. We rented a school bus once and took the whole family to the Detroit Zoo. I'd like to go back to Columbus, Ohio, someday and see what the zoo is like now, after 50 years."

Katie is ready for her trip to Henry's farm. Young John has the horse hitched to the buggy and they stand waiting for her under the old basswood tree. She takes the reins and the horse trots slowly out the farm lane.

Katie and John have 12 children. John tells their names – from the oldest to the youngest – without struggling to remember: Henry, married and farming in Middlesex; Manno, married and farming in Middlesex; Sarah, married Chester Stutzman; Mary married David Stutzman; David is married and farming; Toby is married and farming; Anna married Eddie Yoder; Emma married Andrew Petersheim; Absalom is married and farming; Levi, John and Joni – the ones born in Canada – are living at home.

"We hope our children are safe. We know there are people outside who say *they* are saved. We hope. That is a difference. Ask somebody else and, what I say, you might not get the same answers."

John gets up from his chair. There is work to be done.

6   *Irreplaceable County*

T HERE ARE NO BIG CITIES in Oxford to dilute the impeccable image of good farming country. When the 401 was built across the middle of the county nothing changed much. The old shade trees grew older. The farms got bigger. Woodstock's handsome main residential street became more stately as the first of the three generations retired to enjoy the fruits of being the best dairy farmers in the land.

They made up their minds to be the best. It took three generations of them to do it. It makes them different somehow from the others. Now that they are there at the top, they enjoy staying there. It's hard uncompromising work; but the rewards are obvious. They are the Holstein dairy farmers of Oxford County, the dairy capital of Canada to them.

Their pride in their accomplishment makes Oxford the most beautiful farming county along the 401. The fields, fences, barns, silos, houses and lawns are meticulous. The crossroads villages and market towns are tidy streets of brick and clapboard cottages under old maples and oaks.

Breeding the best Holsteins in the world gives Oxford an international flavour. Buyers fly in from Korea, Venezuela, Ireland, the United States, Mexico, Africa. The Oxford breeders fly to the four corners of the world for national breeders' shows. Natives will admit that there may be more Holstein cattle in

Elmwold Farms Holsteins go to all the beauty contests to win.

Oxford county chorus line.

Perth County; but Oxford wins the production record.

There aren't many of the breeders. Oxford is a small county. When mixed farming – a few cows, a few pigs, some chickens – was the orthodox strategy of southern Ontario, the Oxford dairy men were preaching a gospel of specialization. Today there are 13 counties in Ontario that have more farms than Oxford; but only three of them make more money.

Keith Buchner, in gregarious retirement, tearing up the corn stubble.

Like every county along the 401, Oxford began losing people at the start of the century and in the last 35 years the decline in the number of farm families has been steady.

There is a four-mile stretch along the Brownsville line where once there were 26 prosperous dairy farms with pure-bred Holsteins. Today there are eight. Those that are left are all bigger than any of the old 26 and ship about the same tonnage of whole milk every day as the 26 smaller farms did 35 years ago.

Hooooh ... hooooh ... hoot-hoot. Three times the distant diesel horn blows its melancholy travelling music to warn the unwary at level crossings that a slow freight is on its way. At five-thirty on a dew-drenched morning in May it is an amiable counterpoint to the urgent chirpings of the robins and killdeers swooping into their annual fertility rites in the lush new orchard grass behind the house on the Brownsville line.

The corn harvest.

Keith Buchner imagines the long, slow train drawing its ephemeral line across fields, behind bushes, into cuts and out again and erasing itself as the horn blows more weakly. The train leaves Elgin County, cuts across this corner of Oxford and vanishes into Haldimand. His thoughts roam to public policy issues. It's good to have a cheap-food policy; but there's something amiss when farmers can't afford to buy the butter from the whole milk they produce. He wonders if the Milk Board's television advertising works. Irreplaceable milk.

A minimum wage policy is fine; but does it make sense in a time of high unemployment? British dairy farmers get generous subsidies from their government and that's what wiped out Canadian cheese exports when Britain joined the Common Market. The Americans trump up an excuse to keep Canadian pork out. When dairy farmers produce beyond their quota, they are penalized so the surplus can be marketed abroad in powder form. The cholesterol and triglycerides debate is another problem.

He looks out the kitchen window down the long slope to where the invisible train passed by. Then he glances around him at the trim, spacious ranch bungalow he and Florence designed for themselves. He reflects on mortgage rates, bank rates, quotas, embargos, subsidies, capital gains taxes because, one way or another, he experienced all of them over the years as he worked long hours to create Elmwold Farms on the Brownsville line. He has the time to ponder because he is now the country equivalent of honorary chairman of the board or professor emeritus. He still has the countryman's habit of starting early; but his sons are now the chief executive and chief operating officers of Elmwold Farms. Starting with his inheritance of the family farm from Benona Christopher Buchner, Keith Buchner's irreplaceable wisdom created this big herd of registered Holsteins. Now in gregarious retirement, he has moved all responsibilities on to the next generation.

The next generation has been up since four o'clock. Chris Buchner is on his way to work. Sandra and the three girls are still asleep. The sky is dark. The birds are silent. The dogs semaphore their tails for him as he goes by. The silos and the low barns are familiar shapes darker than the night. The ventilator fans drone lightly.

When he gets there, brother Paul is flushing out the clear pyrex piping system with a mild chlorine and water solution. The 125 Holsteins stand pin-bone to pin-bone in black and white serenity, on rubber mats covered with a thin layer of kiln-dried wood chips. More than three tons of milk wait in their heavily veined udders this morning.

Miss Elmwold Dodie is the cow in the first tie stall on the right as Chris comes in the barn. She has good blood lines. Her daddy was Mississippi Fury and her momma was Elmwold Dora Matt. As usual, Chris rubs her nose as he walks by. She keeps on working her cud. She is used to this kind of passing acknowl-

Chris Buchner disinfects the udder.

edgement. Everybody reaches over to rub her nose when they come in the barn. The special attention makes her a docile performer in the show ring.

Chris straps a one-legged milking stool to his lean behind. The spring in the leg takes the load off his back and feet for the time it takes to disinfect Miss Elmwold Dodie's teats and adjust the four suction cups. The milking unit tugs at the four teats in a rockabilly rhythm. Her milk begins to flow through the black plastic tubes into the Alfa-Laval Mark 4 Milk Meter and then into the two-inch pipeline which takes the milk through the heat transfer and into the bulk tank.

The 125 registered Elmwold Holsteins stand in two rows of tie stalls. Each row of gaunt backsides lines the wide centre aisle of the barn. Paul moves with the same rhythm as Chris to disinfect udders and attach milking units.

The flow of milk from Miss Elmwold Dodie decreases. The measuring device senses it and releases the suction. Chris disinfects her teats again and transfers the unit to Elmwold Wonderful Legacy in the next tie stall. He splashes the disinfectant on Wonderful Legacy, attaches the milking unit and moves on to the next cow.

Elmwold Wonderful Legacy's sire was Roybrook Legacy V.G. V.G. stands for Very Good, which is as close to Excellent as a bull can be. Other sires used by the Buchners at Elmwold Farms are Clinton-Camp Majesty, Hilltopper Warden, Leadfield Prestar, Fair-Breeze Elevation, Glenridge Citamatt, Puget-Sound Sheik, Almerson Rockman Lester, Johanna Senator, Langview Astronaut and Citation R Ex. Ex. stands for excellent.

Wonderful Legacy and Elmwold Dodie don't spend a lot of time bragging to each other about their honourable lineages; but Holstein breeders like the Buchners spend long hours studying the characteristics of the hundreds of bulls available to them through artificial insemination.

Chris, Paul and Glenn – the third generation of Buchners at Elmwold Farms – are together on the lawn for a few minutes. Milking is done. It has been a long day. There will be more just like it all summer long. They talk over tomorrow's plans.

Keith Buchner drives by on the Brownsville road, on his way home. He waves to his sons. They wave and Paul says, "There he goes, the stick and dog man."

Stick and dog man?

"We like to tease him now that he's retired. All he has to do now is get a walking stick and the dog, stroll out to the pasture and see if any of the cows are in heat."

Seven o'clock and Chris is bone weary in his fifteenth hour on the go. A long hot shower will revive him.

While Chris showers, Sandra prepares a dinner of T-bone steaks, fresh asparagus, baked potatoes with butter, ice cream with chocolate chips and milk.

Chris, Sandra and the three girls live in half of the Buchner

Paul disinfects suction unit.

(Right) Nicole and her dad.

family homestead. Paul and his family have the other half.

Chris went to high school in Tillsonburg, then took the two-year certificate course at the University of Guelph. He and Sandra were members of Junior Farmers when they first met. They keep in touch with high-school friends from Tillsonburg. Acquaintances from Junior Farmers days have become their close friends.

Conversation at dinner is easygoing. Sandra thinks she may go into London some day this week. Routine shopping is done

in Tillsonburg. London is for "special" shopping. Sometimes she will go to Kitchener, but never to Toronto. She doesn't like shopping where she doesn't know the stores. She can compare notes on the London stores with friends.

Next weekend will be the long Victoria Day holiday and Chris smiles ruefully. "Friday nights before long weekends, the cars with trailers, boats and campers, that's when I think about the lifestyle of city people." The mild resentment doesn't last long because "we have independence. Ownership is important to us – the reality of what we do. We're 'on call' 24 hours a day even though the three of us take turns being in charge."

"We don't put in a vegetable garden anymore," says Sandra. "During spring planting, haying and harvesting, Chris is going from four in the morning to six-thirty at night and he's in bed by 9:30 most nights. There's just no time left for a garden. It's not the old idea of country life."

The three men have a rotation that gives each of them every other Sunday off. When one of them needs an extra day off, "if you don't put it on the calendar in the barn in advance you don't get it." Chris and Sandra take two weeks off each year and drive to a summer cottage on Long Point. They attend Holstein Association conventions and combine them with some time off.

"We all had the choice of farming or not. I knew in grade twelve that I'd be going back to the farm. Owen had the same choice. He's working for Xerox over in Newmarket."

"It's the combination of responsibilities here that challenges me. There's the health of the animals – 181 cows, heifers and calves. Feeding them for the best yield and keeping accurate records. Running a sanitary operation so we can prevent mastitis and milk fever. Birthing the calves. Planning crops, fertilizer rates, herbicides and pesticides. Maintaining the equipment."

Twelve-year-old Nicole is as tall as twelve-year-old girls should be. Four-year-old Elmwold Martha is as tall as four-year-old Holsteins should be. The ring is crowded with 29 entries in the class.

Once a year the Oxford breeders put on the Holstein show at the Woodstock fairgrounds. This year Nicole Buchner, Chris and Sandy's daughter, makes her first appearance in a show ring, leading Elmwold Martha – a four-year-old dry cow. Keith and Florence Buchner are in the packed bleachers, surrounded by other members of the "Not Quite Over the Hill Gang" – the second-generation crowd whose dairy farming skills are being exhibited by their children and grandchildren. The trick – among others – in showing a pure-bred is to hold a short grip on the lead and urge the cow to keep her head high. This gives her an alert profile. It might be just enough to win the class if the judge glances over when Martha is looking good.

When his scrutiny of each cow is over, the judge lines the cattle up in the order in which they finished, from first to 29th. You need to be philosophical in this business, just in case you and your cow come 29th. Somebody has to.

Elmwold Martha, led by Nicole, came tenth. Not a bad start. Not bad at all.

Lucky lucky white horse.

7   ## The Abandoned Barn

OF ALL THE MEMENTOES of a serene and predictable past, the abandoned barn is the most comforting. The empty barn tells forgotten stories of generations of families.

It sags and settles into the long grass. This year's crop of

burdocks is a pale green man-high palisade around the fieldstone foundation. Nearby, carcasses of dead apple trees decay. The edge of the roof is tattered and frayed. Two blind window holes gape in the south wall. One of the sliding doors was blown off its track by an old March wind.

Inside the barn are the clues of its former utility. The horse-drawn seed drill has faded from Deering red to a venerable pink. It was a once-in-two-lifetimes purchase. A small pile of left-over straw is a remnant of the days when horses and cattle stood and slept in ankle-deep dry bedding that was changed for them every day. Built into the side of a hand-hewn post is a ladder with rungs deeply worn by years of work boots on their way to the hay mow. The doors leading to the passage in front of the horse stalls, down to the cow stable and into the granary have the worn corners and loose-fitting bolts of age. Empty tins that once held axle grease, pine tar and udder balm now rust in a corner. A long-handled pitchfork lies buried in the remains of the hay mow.

Beyond the visible, the abandoned barn shelters innocent histories – children playing on rope swings in the hay mow where the diagonal and dusty sunbeams shine through the barn boards; children shouting to hear their echoes in the empty silo; children using the litter carrier in the cow stable as their private rapid transit; children coasting down the gangway, curry-combing the work horse, making rainy-day forts with granary bin boards, hiding, troubled or giggling, behind the barn.

It is not that people enjoy regret. It is not that people enjoy

signs of decay. The abandoned barn attracts us because it is haunted by the ghosts of real accomplishments. There was the accomplishment of a harvest every year, of animals born and fattened for market. There was the accomplishment of designing and building to last.

Well-built barns take a long time to fall apart and disappear in the tall grass. They were built to endure. They were built to be plainly useful in every season. The abandoned barn comforts us because it kept all the promises it made.

8 *Life in the Clean Lane*

827P looked lovely on her wedding day. Her nose was wet and pink and crinkled appreciatively. Her ear notches were neat and compact. (Some of the others had notches that were so big and sloppy their ears looked like split-leaf philodendrons.)

827P shared a pen with five other females. Life was good to them. Their dainty trotters were clean. Their skin was without blemish. The speakers pumped out good middle-of-the-road rock music from FM96. The food was tasty. The water nipple was at just the right height. What more could she want?

There was a look of lonely importance to 1431R. He lived in the next pen alone. He didn't have to share it with anybody. He had his own water nipple. He had room to pace, room to lie down, spread out and doze the afternoon away. But he paced as though driven by the force in the swollen scrotal sac under his stub tail. With so many females coming and going, there was often an aroma of porcine sexuality.

In the normal course of events he had noticed 827P through

the spaces between the bars. Their noses had touched casually.

This afternoon, the aroma was strong.

Robert Quick stood in the passageway between the rows of pens and looked carefully at each of the females. He let himself into the pen with 827P. He pressed his hands heavily on her back. He butted her flanks with his fists. He leaned heavily on her back again.

"I try to fake her that I'm the boar."

Her responses told him that this could be her day. With light taps on her jowls, he separated 827P from the others and let her out into the passageway. Then he opened the gate into 1431R's pen. She was reluctant and needed a little persuasion to join 1431R.

Alone with 827P at last, 1431R began a brief and decorous courtship. He circled her, grunting contentedly as he smelled her unmistakable aura. She tried to evade his advances because this was her First Time.

1431R was impatient. He began the foreplay: smelling, snuffling, circling, bunting, nuzzling, putting the weight of his head on her back, then putting the weight of his head and one leg on her back. Finally, consummation.

FM96 rocked on. The girls in the next pen paid no attention. 827P and 1431R uncoupled and stared off in opposite directions. Their time together was so short.

"Ciao, eight."

"Ciao, fourteen."

This was no casual one-night stand in some sleazy motel on the edge of town. This was romance foreordained by computerized records of all the mothers, fathers, grandmothers, grandfathers in the genealogy of both 827P and 1431R. It was consummated in the antiseptic pens of a pig barn and a system created by Robert Quick on his farm just east of Bright, where Oxford and Waterloo Counties meet.

827P is a Yorkshire gilt. A gilt is a female pig that has never been bred before. The Yorkshire breed is a desirable strain in market pigs because the Yorkshire sow produces more pigs per litter than other breeds.

1431R is a Landrace boar. The Landrace strain is important in market pigs because Landrace sows have good "mothering" ability. They have lots of milk for the suckling pigs.

Three months, three weeks and three days after their union, 827P – her belly sagging and her teats swollen – will stroll down the hygienically clean corridor to the maternity ward which has been washed and disinfected in readiness for her. Here she will live placidly and comfortably in a farrowing crate – a loose arrangement of metal bars that allows her to stand, sit and lie down in front of her own metal feeding trough and water nipple. The bars are arranged so the newly born pigs can reach the mother's nipples easily; but, at the same time, they prevent the mother pig from rolling over and crushing her babies. The crate arrangement also discourages the mother from turning around and eating her own young.

In each maternity ward there are two rows of six new mothers

Complete physical checkup.

facing each other across a central passageway. The temperature of the ward is kept constant. The doors are kept closed at all times. Visitors to the ward – Bob Quick does not allow many – must wear a clean jumpsuit and must walk through a deep tray of disinfectant before entering the barn. Nobody can get into the barn casually because the doors are locked. Signs warn the un-invited at every entrance.

827P gave birth to 12 piglets. They arrived at 12-minute intervals. One was dead. The remaining 11 – six females and five males – are a Yorkshire–Landrace cross. The Yorkshire–Landrace sow is considered the ideal cross in females for breeding market pigs. That means the six female piglets will get especially careful attention as they grow up because they will be the future mothers of the perfect market pigs. They will be bred to a Hampshire boar (big muscles) or to a Duroc boar (big hams).

The day after the birth day, Bob Quick – jumpsuited and disinfected – goes into the maternity ward with a tray full of

Mealtime in the maternity ward.

instruments and a clipboard. With a pair of stainless steel tooth nippers he deftly nips off the tops of the eight little tusks in the mouth of each piglet. Eventually the roots dry up and fall out. Then he uses a surgeon's scalpel to castrate the males. He snips off the umbilical cord from each piglet and crimps the tail. Each pig gets a shot of iron complex, a shot of vitamins and finally a generous application of disinfectant to the belly button and to the scrotal sac of the males. The females – valuable York–Land-race crosses now – have their ears notched to identify them as the offspring of good old 1431 R and 827 P.

So begin the carefully cloistered lives of 11 piglets. The females will grow up to become super-mothers. The males will end their days as cello-wrapped sacrifices in the refrigerated display altars of the supermarkets.

For a month, momma 827 P stays in the maternity ward with her babies. Then they are weaned from her. Between the birth day and weaning day, she loses two runts that had identical starts in life to their siblings, but for unknown reasons didn't survive.

The original 12 piglets weigh a total of 30 pounds at birth. The nine survivors weigh a total of 200 pounds when they leave their mother for the weaners' parlour.

It was your typical country transaction. George Woolcott decided to buy 25 pigs to fatten. He phoned Bob Quick and they had the usual low-key conversation about the unseasonable weather, the crops and prices. The corn was looking good. A lot of farmers were complaining about the second cut of hay. Not as good as they had hoped; but the barley, wheat and oat crops all turned out real well.

Bob said he would deliver the pigs tomorrow between eleven and noon. As a small friendly gesture, Bob promised he would bring along a couple of frozen lamb chops so the Woolcotts could try them and see what they thought.

Next morning Bob went into the weaners' barn to select the 25 pigs for the Woolcott farm. He lifted each pig easily by one ear and the stub of the tail out of the pen, over the rail and into the weighing crate. The average weight of the pigs was 65 1/2 pounds. From birth it had taken the weaners 10 weeks to reach this weight. In the next 18 weeks each pig would put on another 155 pounds at the Woolcott farm. Then they would be ready for market.

The pigs straggled slowly through the passageway, onto the narrow loading ramp and into the back of the truck. Pigs bred this finely respond acutely to stress, so careful breeders create environments that are as stress-free as possible. Urging the pigs along is done quietly and patiently. Pigs tend to retreat from people; but they come forward when Bob arrives at meal time, they go where he wants them to go. There is no stick, no shouting, no kicking. The old green truck ambles gently down the lane and onto the road to Bright, then north to the Woolcott farm at a sedate 17 miles an hour.

Mealtime in the maternity ward, again.

Bob backs the truck gently to a door at the end of the Woolcott barn. He stops half an inch from the door sill: no sudden impact to throw the pigs off their feet. Done the wrong way, with much kicking and hollering and whacking, delivering pigs can be stressful enough to bring on an outburst of fighting among them, even heart failure. Bob Quick's technique avoids all of that because he guarantees that each pig is going to live for the first week in the new environment. He replaces at no cost pigs that don't survive the change.

The 25 newcomers to the Woolcott farm snuffle their way cautiously off the truck and into their new home.

George uses the hood of his car as a desk and writes the cheque for the pigs. The transaction is almost languid. The conversation follows a serpentine path to the vague end that is good country talk's hallmark.

At last George guesses, artfully, that the lamb chops Bob promised him are probably thawing on the front seat of the truck. Bob looks up into the branches of the trees and asks the Higher Authority whatever happened to his memory. He has forgotten the chops.

"I had them on my mind all morning. I meant to stop at the

55-pound weaners.

house but I was running a little late and I told you I'd be here before noon."

George laughs and decides not to let the subject die a natural death.

"I guess it must be a real burden being married to a man like you, forgetting things like that. I feel sorry for Linda. I think I'll just send her a little bouquet of roses. Do you think she'd like them?'' He clips the roses and snips the thorns off the stems as deftly as Bob nipped the teeth out of the baby pigs yesterday.

Suitably humbled, Bob puts the roses on the truck seat and drives down the Woolcott Lane and back to the farm.

At lunchtime, Linda asks, ''Did you deliver the pigs to the Woolcotts?''

''Mm-hmm.''

''How did it go?''

He hands her the half-dozen roses.

''I wish you hadn't asked.''

Sheep are a sideline at the Robert Quick farm.

Father and Son Country

WHEN A COUNTRY BOY decides he wants to carry on in his father's tradition, the decision raises questions in his father's mind.

Did my son decide he wants to stay on the farm because it is comfortable, familiar and secure? Is it because he knows these risks and is afraid of the unknown ones he'll face in doing something else?

Do I really want him to follow in my footsteps? I am successful; will he be? Or will he be betrayed by markets, the weather, interest rates or something unforeseeable? Or, I haven't been all that successful and now I'm too old to take on the new technologies. Will two years at an agricultural college guarantee he'll do better than I did?

I wonder if he's been away from home enough to have some perspective on farming life. I wonder if we kept him from trying out other choices. Have I been putting some kind of subtle pressure on him because I want him to carry on after me? Is that fair?

Well, he's definitely made up his mind. How are we going to work out things so that we're both happy doing what needs doing on the farm? Will the Farm Credit Corporation lend him money in his own name? Will I ever learn how to say "my son's farm"? That's going to take a while.

The country boy has another list of questions. He's been going to a big school in town all these years and he's made friends with lots of non-farm people in a way that his father didn't. He knows classmates who have gone on to law, dentistry, business administration.

Would I make a good chartered accountant? Maybe I'd be a good teacher. Who would want to marry anyone chained to a dairy farm? A regular paycheque with pension deductions makes a lot of sense. Sometimes.

Gradually answers come to both sets of questions. If I kept up with the changes in farming for 30 years do I want to keep on keeping up? The changes won't stop coming. Maybe I want to stop. My son will have a jump on the future after the two year dip. course at the agricultural college.

I know what salary plus commission is. I know what little houses in big cities cost. My friends complain now about not being able to build up much of an equity in anything. Oh, they've the money to spend on Trans-ams and nursery schools for the kids and trips overseas and they say they play the stock market a little, but they don't feel they own anything. The principal on the mortgage never seems to get any smaller.

Ownership. Owning where you grew up. Owning what your father built up after he inherited it from Grandpa. It has to do with permanence. A farm is a farm – except this farm has been in our family for more than 125 years.

Wood Creek is as muddy as ever but not running quite as deep as it did during the Spring runoff. Malcolm and Andrew Condie cross the road and take a possessive look at the 70 acres of corn that is now close to a foot high. Last week's rain was perfect.

Barry, Rod and Miller Grant, Stormont County.

The parallel rows converge on a vanishing point down near Bainsville. Andrew will be going into his last year at Alexandria in September. After that he hopes for the two-year course at Kemptville. Then decisions will be made.

The dark green foliage along the course of Wesleys Creek is home for goldfinches, song sparrows and red-winged blackbirds. Across the road at Heidi Farms, the Oeggerlis – Paul and young Paul – put in long hours in an atmosphere of pride. It is only 15 years ago that Paul and Heidi put the down payment on the farm. Now, young Paul has his diploma from Kemptville. He runs the computerized supplementary feeding system for the Holsteins. The artificial inseminations he was responsible for "took." He helps his father string a temporary electric fence so they can

move the heifers from the home farm to the one next door. The decision has been made.

The South Raisin River is only a creek when it curls east around the Grant barns. Millard Grant is running the riding mower on the lawn around his new brick bungalow. One of his sons, Rod, is on the far side of the creek seeing how a cow and her newborn

Kenneth, Earl and Brie Elgie, Kent County.

Chris and Keith Buchner, Oxford County.

calf are getting along. The grandchildren are off to school in the yellow bus. His other son, Barry, is in the machine shop. Wagons, tractors and hay harvesters will be readied this week for the first cut of the haying season. The milk truck will be along in a little while. Millard, Barry and Rod meet outside the milking parlour. Marlboro men with brains. Good partnership decisions were made here a few years ago.

At Prescott where the St. Lawrence flows wider and deeper than the Thames, the Rhone, the Rhine, the Missouri or the Ohio, the day's work is done. Hubert Casselman puts the hard hat back on the shelf. His son, Kevin, drops into the office for some small talk. Kevin bought a small piece of land back in the country near where he was born. The house was finished last year. Although they don't look much like each other, the father and son share strong feelings of independence, the need for a certain separation from urban life.

The waters of Popham Bay, formed by the lakeshore and the west side of Presqu'Ile, are a strong, sparkling blue. The wind is up. Maybe it's too windy to spray the new orchard across the road from the motel. Maybe not. Paul Chatten puts the blue face mask on and turns the tractor out of the yard, down the shallow ditch to the new orchard. His father, Earle, is in bed with a terrible cold. It is going to be one of those weeks. "And this is another week that started a day late because I was at directors' meetings in Guelph on Sunday and Monday," Paul says. He lets out the clutch and an $800 mix of fungicide, pesticide and water swirls out of the sprayer and shrouds the new trees in a dense white mist. Another decision has been made.

Down at the mouth of Wilmot Creek, Steve Selby is spraying the 90 acres of corn with a mix of liquid nitrogen and herbicide. The self-levelling sprayer on the back of the tractor is a pain in the butt. The spray nozzles clog up too often and have to be cleared. Back at the home farm, Newt Selby has taken a 30-minute nap before he goes out to deliver the rotary orchard mower to a neighbour just getting started in apples. Newt speaks openly and with pride of how fond the Selbys are of Steve's wife. Steve comes into the yard on the tractor. The sprayer is up in the transport position. "I wonder what that's all about," Newt says.
    Something is wrong with the sprayer. Newt follows the tractor into the machine shop. There is a brief, knowing conversation.

Steve sets to work. Newt jumps into the pick-up and he's gone. Another partnership.

It is past midnight. The lights are on at Keith and Florence Buchner's. They are just back from the Woodstock fairgrounds. A first and two seconds. Very good. Down the road at the home farm, Chris, Paul and Glenn back the truck to the barn door. The nine Holsteins step warily out of the truck like eight-year-olds wearing their mother's high-heeled shoes. It has been a long day, but a first and two seconds – a good day.

Out on the black muck of the Marenpettit Marsh, Walter is on one onion harvester, son Robert is on the other. They creep slowly along to the end of the quarter-mile rows. Prices could be better, but the yield looks good. It's going to be a fine year for Cherneski and Sons, Onions.

10   *Nailed Down*

At last the image of southwestern Ontario comes into focus.

From the porch of the 1860 Lucas house in the Ontario Agricultural Museum, the CN Tower is a distant exclamation mark, a skinny thumb-tack holding down this midpoint of the 401.

Everybody who visits the museum near Milton has a farm background. They are mostly retired farm families who have good memories of their early childhood on the farm. The first person they meet at the museum is Mr. Clark, the cashier, who was born on a farm near St. Mary's 65 years ago. He guides them to the sight-seeing wagon to be carried on a sedate circuit of the barns, fields and reconstructions. The window of memory is wide open and the memories come flooding in.

Albert Fyfe is in charge of the ancient tractors and threshing machines. Each day he selects a Rumley or a high old Sawyer Massey and takes it on a one-mile-per-hour circuit of the museum, just to keep the old pistons and valve lifters in shape and to give the visitors a touch of the clumsy past. Then the graceful young people in their period costumes talk to the visitors about the summer kitchen, the old stoves, the day bed and the wall-paper, and finally offer a molasses cookie or a slice of bread.

At every moment, somewhere in the museum, a voice calls out in remembrance.

"I bought the first self-propelled combine in our area. I paid

three thousand two hundred dollars." The taut-cheeked pensioner is quietly pleased to find the model on display.

"There's the one and a half horsepower stationary engine that took the place of our windmill. The very one."

"We had a deacon's bench on our porch just like that one."

Templin's Carriage and Waggon Works is a nexus of health and quiet. It has been decided that the visitors to the museum would prefer a horse-drawn wagon for sightseeing, instead of one pulled by a tractor. It has also been decided that the team of

Percherons are overweight and don't get enough exercise. So the short tractor tongue on the wagon is being replaced by a long tongue to let the fat Percherons take over and lose a little weight.

In the Methodist church that was moved here from Mayne Corners, the needlepoint treadles on the organ are faded and frayed; but the finely turned spindle rails and candleholders are nicely polished. The rack that holds the hymn numbers shows that hymn number six was sung at the last service. A 1930 edition of the *United Church of Canada Hymn Book* sits in the back of every pew. The last line of hymn number six is the museum's creed: "When rolling years shall cease to move."

The trip is done.